CONFLICT UNRAVELED
Fixing Problems
at Work and in Families

by Andra Medea

Please visit our website at **www.PivotPointPress.com** for more information.

Library of Congress Cataloging-in-Publication Data
Medea, Andra, 1953– . Conflict Unraveled: Fixing Problems at Work and in Families / by Andra Medea. - 1st Edition [p. cm.]
Includes bibliographical references and index.

Library of Congress Control Number: 2003112609

ISBN 0-9745808-0-5

Cover/Design by Su Strong

Dedicated to
Dr. Bonny Flaster
who was determined to see
this book come to life.

Table of Contents

Conflict baffles everyone. Conflict is strange and confusing, frustrating and contrary, and comes without a set of instructions. Whether at work, at home or visiting the step-kids, conflict makes no sense, goes on and on and will not stop when you want it to.

But perhaps all that can change.

This book is the result of fourteen years of development, with field testing in classes I taught at Northwestern, DePaul and now the University of Chicago. This approach finds the logic underneath conflict, shows the hidden forces at work and then points out some unexpected ways to handle it.

It's not that conflict doesn't make sense; it just makes a different kind of sense than what we were expecting.

The key to this new approach is the conflict continuum, which spells out how a conflict changes as power is misused. What solves reasonable conflict will have little effect on a conflict gone wrong. This book shows how to tell the difference and what to do about it.

Since conflict affects nearly everything that involves human behavior this system can be used for a great many things. Professional problem-solvers such as mediators and lawyers find that it gives them the ability to quickly gauge a situation and map a course of action. At the Oxford University Press the black women historians saw that my model could highlight hidden currents and so tapped me to write about civil rights and sexual harassment.

However, much of my work has been showing regular people how to solve everyday problems. Couples find they can get past old issues, parents find they can better come to terms with their teen-agers and businesspeople find they can manage both bosses and subordinates more effectively.

In this book I've focused on the problems close to home: you, your job and your family. The material is professional strength but you don't have to be an expert to do this. In fact, it may help that you're not. Kids master computers faster than accountants do because they have less to unlearn. They come in fresh, without preconceptions, and are happily hacking away while veteran CPAs are still cursing at their monitors.

This book is based on the idea that different kinds of conflicts operate by different rules. This means that you have not been crazy all along. In the past you may have tried sensible things to solve a conflict and gotten nowhere at all. That wasn't because you were foolish, inept or secretly wanted to fail. It means that you tried the right technique on the wrong kind of conflict, and failed as surely as if you had tried to treat malaria with penicillin. Malaria doesn't respond to penicillin; malaria is treated with quinine. Match the treatment to the problem and you will get much better results.

The book is arranged from more basic to more sophisticated techniques. If your concern is solid good management or good parenting, you'll be primarily interested in the first seven chapters of this book. If your company is going through a tumultuous merger or your exasperating in-laws move in with you, look to the harder cases towards the back of the book. Even if you're tempted to skip to the most difficult parts, please look over the earlier chapters first. The harder chapters build on the easier ones, and if you're going to learn mountain climbing it's best not to start in the Himalayas.

While much of this book comes from my own system, I've had the pleasure of showcasing techniques that should be mandatory for the human race. Some of these techniques are not commonly known, while others were in danger of being forgotten entirely. They were developed by some of the finest minds in the field.

There are the brain and adrenaline studies developed by John Gottman, and the primate studies of Frans DeWaal. Nanci Newton of Chimera self-defense used primate behavior to short-circuit violence. Deborah Tannen, a best selling author, took the best practices from linguistics and translated them for the general public.

One of the most exciting aspects of this project was finding new uses for tactical non-violence. Diane Nash and James Bevel did some of their most famous work together back in the civil rights movement, but have since developed along different lines. More of Bevel's work is presented here, but I hope that Nash will continue to expand her techniques and share them with the planet.

While many of the non-violent activists are viewed solely as historic figures, many are still alive and have a great deal to say about issues in the here and now. We need to capture their wisdom while they're still with us.

Joel Barker developed groundbreaking work on paradigm theory, the science of new ideas, along with the practical applications that are so crucial to the modern world. This project, as a new idea, could have never happened without his research.

Corrine "Cookie" Levitz is a veteran with the Cook County Mediators who pushes the envelope of problem-solving and what mediation can do. Her work and that of her colleagues at the Center for Conflict Resolution have helped make Chicago a center for innovation and excellence.

Barbara Fleming is an unusual and gifted counselor, who explained some of the more puzzling self-perpetuating patterns.

Pam Woll is a writer who documents the cutting edge of addiction studies, who was an invaluable source on developments in the field of addiction and recovery.

Apart from the specialists, there are others to thank as well. Many of the examples in this book are from students at Northwestern or DePaul Universities, who produced some remarkable projects.

Kathleen Thompson proved invaluable, as always, for her insights and encouragement over the years.

Marjorie Butterworth was a formidable critic, making her points with convincingly bad language.

Robert Logan, the editor, was as thoughtful and astute as any writer could desire.

Kendra Reinshagen, now head of her division with the Legal Assistance Foundation, helped start this process long ago by asking the right questions at the right time.

My mother, Emily Thomas, a charming and intelligent woman, was perhaps the most skilled person at breaking up fights I've ever seen in action.

My good friend and advisor V., who wishes to remain anonymous, contributed infinite encouragement.

Su Strong created an elegant design and cover for the book itself, fielding changes while somehow keeping her sense of humor.

And finally I have to thank Linus the medical student from Michigan, whose trials with the med school establishment finally pushed me to get this book to press.

In most of the following cases, identifying names and details have been changed to protect the innocent and the guilty alike.
A few cases have been combined for the sake of brevity.
Any errors in interpretation of studies are entirely my own, and do not reflect on the researchers cited.

– A.M.

Chapter One

Adrenaline Overload: Flooding

You may have noticed that people stop making sense when they fight. Sound, cooperative, intelligent people stop acting like themselves and do inexplicable things. They kill projects they love, walk away from people they care about and get into furious arguments over last year's tomato plants.

Barring a takeover by an alien life force, something happens to make reasonable people act this way. It's called flooding.

Flooding is an adrenaline overload that was the subject of landmark research by Dr. John Gottman and later, psychologists Kim Buehlman and Lynn Katz. Flooding shorts out most of the higher parts of the brain and leaves people acting irrational, mule-headed, defensive or quarrelsome.

People are roughly familiar with this as the 'flight-or-flight' syndrome, but Gottman and his associates have taken this concept much farther. By using sophisticated equipment they have been able to pin down exactly how the brain is misfiring and how that translates to human behavior.

In short, the problem is not character, but chemical. And the first step in managing conflict is to be braced for this chemical onslaught, because it will undermine every other useful skill you own.

Here's what it looks like:

Glen is trapped in his office by an abrasive woman who is always pushing for something *more*:

"I feel an accelerating heart-beat and a flushing in my face. My mind seems to go completely blank. I simply forget to think. This seems to be caused by an urge from within to do or say anything that will get this woman away from me. I have suffered from this in the past, and made decisions and issued instructions that I later lived to regret..."

Tessa comes homes early to find her teenaged step-son, who is supposed to be in school, making out with his girlfriend in full view of all the neighbors:

"Rigidity, locked knees, clenched fists, and grinding of teeth... a racing heartbeat... I have too many thoughts, all wanting to be expressed immediately... Logic seems to have vanished... And I can't remember what I wanted to say after I start talking."

Cal hit a computer glitch and had to seek help from the dreaded tech staff:

"I struggled for computer vocabulary. Now I really felt like a fool and my face began to turn red. Every icon looked like a blur of color. I could not distinguish which icon I used every day for the past year. I was being perceived as an idiot but I knew what I was talking about and this made me more angry. I couldn't think clearly after that moment. My reasoning and logic skills were nowhere to be found..."

Cindy's boyfriend calls ten minutes to deadline, after she's repeatedly asked him not to call on deadline days:

"...all I can see is red. My blood rushes all at once to the top of my head and my eyes seem to glaze over. My heart is beating faster than I've ever known or realized it could, and I feel like I'm losing control, because I can't hear anything my boyfriend is saying... I feel hot and it feels like the walls are closing in on me, almost like a claustrophobic person would feel in an enclosed place..."

These were intelligent, effective people who found themselves so upset they couldn't think or speak or function. Like stage fright, it's an entirely human reaction. It isn't stupidity, weakness or an incipient nervous breakdown, but the normal result of flooding. Flooding short-circuits the higher parts of the brain, like logic, speech and judgment, which leaves people stranded in bad situations without the very skills they need to get out again.

When you're desperately trying to explain yourself and find yourself babbling like a fool, that's flooding. If you're dashing out the door and can't find your keys—even though they're lying right in front of you- that's flooding. When you can't face seeing your ex-wife, your boss or your father-in-law, even though you've done nothing wrong and they happen to be trying to help you, when the sound of a certain set of footsteps can make the lungs seize up in your chest, that's flooding. It's normal, it's human and it can be controlled.

Flooding happens to everyone sometime, and to many of us as a regular event. Controlling flooding becomes top priority in conflict management, because flooding will undercut every other rational skill you own.

Flood control can be done by anyone, barring an active psychosis. First you need to recognize flooding when it hits; the sooner you recognize it, the less power it will have over you. Next, know its hazards: know what flooding does and what you need to watch for, both in yourself and others. Finally, at a quiet time, create a personal plan you can use under stress to head off flooding so it won't hijack your brain.

The object of the game is to control flooding rather than letting it control you.

Recognizing Flooding

The physical symptoms are easiest to spot. Your heart speeds up, or your breathing goes tight. Your head starts pounding as your blood pressure rises: it may feel like a headache or a tourniquet tightening around your skull. Your face may flush and your skin feel hot; fair skinned people turn red, while dark skinned people get darker. Your mouth may go dry in a 'cottonmouth' feeling, or your palms break into a sweat. A few people get a 'pins and needles' sensation in their fingers and toes. Muscles tense as your brain shuts down.

This was a person being yelled at by her boss:

"It was as if all my fluids had turned to solids and my body would snap in half if I were to bend over. Then my thinking stopped, as if I were going into a shell to hide while the attack was taking place..."

Physical symptoms are relatively easy to spot, while mental symptoms are harder to recognize. This is because flooding blocks the higher parts of the brain, even as it overstimulates the lower, more reptilian parts. The reptilian brain isn't capable of recognizing spotty thinking, which may explain a good deal of local and national politics. However, the reptile brain can recognize physical changes and raw emotion. You may never notice when you've stopped making sense, but you'll notice if you can't get the words out.

Check for raw emotion: Do you feel trapped or claustrophobic? Furious or provoked? Do you feel like you're losing your mind? Everyone has a different pattern, and it's important for you to know your individual symptoms.

As a rule, if someone else is flooding, check to see if you're flooding, too. Flooding is contagious: it can spread to you without your noticing. Now, it may seem as if the most important thing is to get the other person to stop flooding In fact, it's much more important that you get your brain back first. Worry about the other person later. It's like the oxygen mask in the airplane: you have to put on your own mask first or you won't last long enough to help anyone else. First you control your own flooding, and only then are you ready to handle anyone else. Flooding may be contagious, but then so is calm.

Silent Flooding

Some people explode under stress; others pull in and barricade. People who flood silently show few outward symptoms, they just do things that make no sense. They shut up, clamp down and won't respond, even to defend themselves.

Two co-workers regularly set each other off, and when they were together in a meeting Mary would inevitably anger John. But John wouldn't counterattack; he would pull back, turn red and silently study his fingernails. He would not say another word, which meant, essentially, that the meeting was over.

This would infuriate Mary, who also would start flooding. No silent type, Mary would make some scathing remark and John would still say nothing. Fury would ripple through the room while the other team members pretended not to notice. The meeting would be rescheduled, because they still had their work to accomplish, and when they got back together the same thing would happen all over again.

Mary may seem unreasonable, but her response was fairly typical. When faced with silent flooding, many people are seized with the desire to provoke a reaction. They think: "Ignore me, will you? I'll give you something you can't ignore."

Someone who is silently flooding is not ignoring you. In fact, they're hyper-aware; they're just not able to react. They won't be able to react until they calm down, so you may as well decrease the pressure. Lower your voice, don't raise it. Leave space, don't crowd. Lean back, not forward. This person is much more upset than you think. Give them a chance to calm down. Later they may be able to deal with you.

Incidentally, women are more likely to stay verbal while flooding, while men are more likely to do the silent shut-down. Studies indicate that women often prefer to keep talking to hash things through, while men may desperately wish to be left alone. Actually, this isn't necessarily a good time to talk; it may be wiser to be quiet and separate. A good many marriages could benefit from this.

Flooding in Action

With enough flooding, people do inexplicable things. Mike, a sales manager, got upset when he saw a staggering bill from a messenger service and ordered everyone but his own secretary to stop using the service. A few days later Phil, the star sales rep, needed to make a rush delivery.

Now, there had been bad blood between the manager and Phil, because the sales rep's paychecks were often bigger than his boss's. So rather than cause a stir, the boss's secretary and Phil's secretary quietly conspired to send the package by messenger. They didn't tell anyone, not even Phil, and thought the boss would never find out. He did.

Mike, thinking that his authority had been flaunted, flew into a rage. Phil, however, had never been told what the secretaries had done. As Mike screamed at him in the middle of the office, Phil kept repeating that he didn't know what Mike was talking about, but the manager kept shouting and crowding him. Phil, who was now bright red, kept backing away and repeating himself. Mike was openly flooding, but Phil was silently flooding. The boss failed to notice that he was not only having an effect, he was pushing the salesman towards the edge.

The boss's secretary—who actually made the shipment—kept trying to explain, but everyone ignored her. Finally, to get his attention she caught her boss's arm; he pushed her away, but since he was pumped with adrenaline, she went flying. Seeing his boss hit a woman, Phil snapped, grabbed Mike by the throat and started choking him. The rest of the office jumped in to pull them apart. Once the salesman was pulled off his boss he was horrified at what he'd done. Suddenly lucid, he backed away with his arms down, shaking.

Mike was equally dumbfounded: he'd just knocked his own secretary across the room. The secretaries now rushed in to explain, but both Mike and Phil were so shaken they could barely follow it. All they knew was that Phil hadn't made the shipment, Mike had swung on his own secretary, and they'd just tried to kill each other.

From that point forward, both Mike and Phil were studiously polite and careful with each other. They didn't know what happened; they only knew they never wanted anything like that to happen again.

Don't make fast moves around people who are flooding. Don't catch their arm, don't jump too close. Flooding people are highly reactive and can snap without knowing what they're doing. Don't crowd them. Leave space. You might get more of a reaction than you had in mind.

Losing the Ability to Hear New Information

Mike didn't respond when Phil said he didn't send the package, he just kept shouting. And it wasn't only the sales rep he ignored—he paid no attention when two different secretaries told him the same thing. But this boss wasn't just being difficult: under flooding, people lose their ability to take in information.

You've seen this yourself: "When he gets mad, there's no talking to that guy." "She gets like this and there's nothing I can say." "I've already explained it five times over. What does it take to get through to you?" These people aren't just being provoking. They can't hear you. Flooding shuts off the part of the brain that can take in new information.

In a laboratory scientists were connected to skin monitors and brought to a state of flooding, then presented with new information. Not only did they not register the new data, but their *skin* didn't behave as if new information had entered the room. Their brains literally could not take it in.

You may have found yourself in the surreal position of agreeing with someone who's yelling at you, saying everything she could want to hear, and still have her keep shouting as if you disagreed. You offer her a refund, a new computer or a free trip to China: it makes no difference. She's still arguing because she can't hear you. And very quickly, you can expect to be flooding as well.

Once both sides are flooding, for all intents and purposes the conversation is already over. It's time to call it a day. Respectfully say you'll get back to her; be clear and set a time and place, but stop talking and close the conversation. Some people have been known to suddenly develop problems with the telephone line. It helps explain the popularity of cell phones.

Before this person can hear your offer, she has to stop flooding. Your only chance to get her to stop flooding is for you to stop flooding first. Here's how it's done.

Flood Control: Working Large Muscles

The fastest way to stop flooding is by working large muscle groups, such as arms, legs, shoulders or torso. Large muscle exercise works so well—and is so automatic—that I suspect a chemical catalyst at work. Whatever it is, large muscle action triggers something that washes out flooding and clears the mind.

Sometimes the change is so abrupt that people look as if they've had a personality transplant. One man in a rage put his fist through a wall, then thoughtfully noted, "Well, that was a stupid thing to do." It was as if the man who put his hand into the wall and the one who pulled his hand out were two different people, only one of them needed to go to the emergency room.

For a less painful solution, close the door to your office and do ten jumping jacks. If your head doesn't clear, do ten more. Take a fast walk around the block; an easy stroll won't do it. Whatever you choose, keep it up until your brain starts to clear, and *then* go back and contend with the problem.

There are times—say in meetings—when it isn't possible to step outside or drop to the floor for a few quick sit-ups. If you can't leave the room, do isometrics. Slip your hands out of sight and try to lift the table. (It may feel, at times, as if you could heave the whole thing straight against the wall. You can't.) Push your elbows against the arm rests; try to lift your own chair. Any kind of isometrics will do, as long as it uses large muscle groups. Meanwhile, keep breathing.

Flood Control: Breathing

Since one of the signs of flooding is quick, shallow breathing, it's helpful to deliberately reverse the symptoms. Force yourself to take deep, slow breaths.

Luther was a school superintendent who was going to do a favor for Sarah, who promptly stood him up for the meeting. After half an hour, Luther angrily reached for the phone to read her off, but as he reached over he realized his head was throbbing and his mouth was dry. He was flooding.

Luther put the phone back down. Wanting to collect himself, he walked up and down the hall, breathing deeply until his head cleared. Then he went back in his office and called.

It was just as well he had taken that walk, because Sarah had been delayed handling a crisis that later earned her a commendation. Luther had been so angry he would have exploded without waiting for any explanation.

Flooding often makes you feel as if you must react right then, that very instant. In fact, you seldom need to. It's wiser instead to take a moment and handle the flooding first. Nothing is lost by a few moments' silence, even in the middle of a heated argument. The other side isn't listening to you anyway and you can disengage for quite a while before they even notice that you've stopped talking.

Flood Control: Concentrating on Facts or Details

Another technique is to focus in on individual facts. Flooding will make your thinking scrambled and chaotic; by slowing down the action and forcing yourself to concentrate on details, you force your brain to keep functioning.

Maureen managed sales reps who worked on commission. They were inclined to close sales at any cost, while Maureen had to double-check the contracts to make sure the terms were realistic.

The sales reps were primed to blast through any opposition, and Maureen was one more barrier to be blasted. After eight hours of fighting with sales reps she found herself rubber-stamping contracts out of sheer exhaustion.

Once Maureen realized the sales reps had her flooding, she created a plan. First she let the sales rep state the case without interruption, while she concentrated on her breathing. She'd write down each fact, tuning out the pressure and forcing her brain to stay engaged.

After the sales rep had finished, Maureen went down her list and double-checked each fact. She deliberately slowed the momentum and the sales rep slowed with her. Maureen then asked a few questions, still taking careful notes. Only then would she give her decision. If the sales rep didn't like her answer Maureen would take the same careful notes on the disagreement. If the points seemed valid, Maureen promised to call the rep back later, but only after she had time to walk around, breathe and clear her head.

After Maureen used this system for a few weeks, she noticed three things had changed. First, phone calls no longer started on the attack. Second, she found that the sales reps were far less likely to challenge her decisions and go over her head to her boss. Third, her working relationships had become more relaxed and she was no longer going home with pounding headaches.

A collections agent developed his own technique. He was immune to routine abuse, but every now and then someone would start to get to him; he'd then tune out the anger and focus on his desk.

While the stranger stormed he would pick up a pen and describe it to himself: "Blue ballpoint pen, with silver band and etched black logo." He would feel the smoothness of the barrel and test the weight in his hand. Then he would put the pen down exactly where he found it and repeat the process with a paperclip or stapler. He would go over every object on his desk until he felt himself get grounded again.

Flooding as a Feedback Loop

Flooding, left to its own devices, tends to go into a self-reinforcing cycle. The first burst of adrenaline blocks the higher brain centers and stimulates the lower parts. Being aroused—and not very bright—the lower brain handles the problem by calling for more adrenaline. This, of course, further blocks the higher centers and further arouses the lower parts. And so on.

After a while, flooding takes on a life of its own. Families, even business groups, learn to fight in shorthand. Someone mentions "Desiree" or "April shoes," and the whole group starts flooding. Outsiders may watch amazed, never knowing what it's all about.

Thinking Problems: Logic and Sequence

With flooding, logic disappears in a jumble of chaotic thoughts. Sometimes there are only two or three thoughts frantically running in an endless loop. This may feel logical, but it's not. A clear mind would be bored silly after the first few times around the track.

As part of this breakdown people lose the ability to do sequence. This is why it's so exasperating to listen to someone who's very upset. The flooding person rambles, stumbles, doubles-back, makes wild accusations then brings up something that happened years ago. After five solid minutes and a pounding headache you still don't know what happened. Remember, flooding tends to be contagious, so as this person loses the ability to explain, you lose your ability to follow the story. By the end your head is throbbing, you no longer care and you just wish he'd go away.

Difficulty with sequence actually can be used to help pull someone else out of flooding. Keep your voice low and calm, then ask simple sequence questions: "What happened first?" "Is that what happened next?" Or even "Could you please spell your name?"

I've seen people flooding so badly they couldn't manage to spell their own names. It shocked them and they directly pulled themselves together. Any simple sequence will do, including order numbers, timing or any kind of code number.

I once came across a man who had cracked his head open in a bicycle accident, who kept struggling to get up before the ambulance came. There were people on hand to help, but he was clearly flooding and no one could convince him to stay where he was. Instead of arguing, I asked him to count from one to ten. When that was done, I asked him to count from ten to one, backwards. This was so difficult—and demanded such concentration—he did it over and over until help arrived, calming down as he did so.

One customer service rep realized that she failed to consider flooding when she talked to upset clients. She might offer someone a refund, yet often they'd go right on yelling. Of course they were flooding and couldn't hear the information, so the offer did no good. Arguing back was clearly pointless, so she'd take them through sequence questions. She'd ask for their address, their phone number, and go down a list of questions. All the while, she'd listen for their voice to get calmer and their statements to become more coherent. Once they had calmed down, *then* she'd make her offer and then it would be accepted.

Loss of Options

Under flooding, options disappear. This can be very serious, especially with young people. Jack says to Harry: "Harry, put that gun down! That wasn't me with your girlfriend!" But Harry can't hear this new information and he just might pull the trigger.

Harry's heart is crashing, and his head feels like it's going to explode. For that moment in time, it feels like Harry *has* to shoot Jack. If no failsafe mechanism is in place to stop him, it's quite possible for Harry to shoot because he can't think of anything else to do.

While flooding, people feel they must do something and they can think of only one thing: Quit. Sue. Walk out of the marriage. That single choice may be incredibly foolish, but if it's the one thing they think of it can be the one thing they do.

Thinking Problems: Speech and Simple Tasks

Flooding can make normal people talk as if they were brain-impaired: "That was—was—stupid! That was just—could—Stupid!" Actually, flooding blocks the pathways leading from the speech centers in the brain; you may feel you have all sorts of things to say, but not be able to get the words out.

If you can only choke out one word, say: "Later." It does explain something and it won't get you fired or divorced.

Because the language centers are badly affected, jargon can make people extremely hostile. You may have experienced this yourself with a computer breakdown. Someone starts firing questions in data-speak, and you suddenly want to rip his heart out; yet this is someone trying to help you. It doesn't matter: you wish to kill him. For that matter, you can unwittingly provoke the same reaction in someone else who doesn't know *your* jargon.

As you might expect, flooding will demolish math skills. Remember this the next time you sit down to do your income taxes. Meanwhile, never yell at people who are doing math for you. If they're trying to straighten out a bill, flooding will only make things worse.

A graphics manager was amazed to realize her team's error rate doubled whenever they had a periodic rush. What was worse, the errors were obvious typos and were concentrated in the work of their most volatile client. She hadn't known about flooding; she thought this behavior was fear of success or some kind of death-wish.

Between problems with listening and inability to do sequence, flooding can make it nearly impossible to follow directions. Every family has been through this.

Dad's up on a ladder, fixing the ceiling light. Katie, his kid, is on the ground to help. Dad wrestles with the fixture, jams his finger, swears a blue streak and barks at Katie to get him the red Phillips-head screwdriver from the basement.

But flooding's contagious. Katie dashes to the basement, sees the tools and goes blank: What was she supposed to get? A screwdriver? Maybe yellow?

She stands there paralyzed, not knowing what to do. She can't go back and ask Dad because he'll bite her head off, but she also can't figure out what she should do. So she grabs a bunch of tools, all of which are wrong and some of which aren't even screwdrivers.

Dad sees the jumble and throws an absolute fit. What the hell is wrong with this kid? She can't even listen to simple directions.

Nothing's wrong with the kid. This isn't sabotage or passive-aggression; it's a simple flooding breakdown.

The business version is when a manager badgers an employee into flooding, barks a string of orders and then becomes livid when the directions aren't followed. The boss thinks he's surrounded by idiots, while the employees wish he'd go away and calm down so they could get some work done.

Flooding Problems: Suggestibility

People become highly suggestible while flooding. Be careful what you say.

Eric was playing tennis while Alice watched. Eric kept missing his shots and the other side teased him unmercifully. The more upset he got, the more they teased him and the worse his game got. Flooding gave him strength but no judgment; he couldn't get the muscle release because he couldn't get a volley going before the next barrage of jeers and catcalls.

Alice knew Eric was flooding because his shots were wild and his face had gone dark red. She went over and quietly explained about flooding, and suggested he'd feel better if he did some large muscle movement. Eric said, "Yes!" and smashed his tennis racket.

Flooding people will even take suggestions from their worst enemy. The hated boss says to the analyst, "If you don't like it here, why don't you quit?" The analyst answers, "You're right, I quit." If this analyst truly disliked and distrusted his boss, it would be better to take suggestions from someone else.

Choose your words carefully around flooding people. During a down-sizing a bank VP reported to the CEO that they couldn't make any more cuts—unless they wanted to do something crazy like cut international finance. That was a prize profit center that had taken years to assemble. The CEO snapped, "Cut it!" The VP desperately tried to talk him out of it, but the CEO was no longer listening. The rest of his options had disappeared. This, in turn, panicked the rest of the staff, who felt that management was out of control.

Finally, flooding people routinely say things that don't bear scrutiny from functional intelligence. Should anyone ever say to you, "You can't speak to me that way!" stop immediately and try to remember what you just said. If you can't remember, odds are they're right. Stop, re-group and apologize.

Flooding as a Learned Reaction

Flooding is learned in a roughly Pavlovian way. If you flooded the last few times you saw Thor, your toughest client, you're likely to flood next time you see him. This can happen even if Thor does nothing whatsoever beside walk into the room. Your brain has learned: Thor = flooding, and your thinking will short-circuit accordingly.

This learned reaction can be put to good use. Since the brain is trained to learn flooding, you can also train it to un-learn the reaction.

Helen, an entrepreneur, flooded whenever she saw her loan officer. The man drove her crazy and she only needed to think about his voice to feel the walls closing in.

Helen deliberately worked with that reaction. She had a meeting coming up, so she sat at her desk and imagined the loan officer's voice, then jotted down her reactions: heart racing, short breathing, dry mouth, jumbled thinking, etc. Then she'd jog in place until she felt coherent again.

As she worked on her proposal, Helen checked her reactions and started jogging whenever she started to flood. She ended up with a better proposal in considerably less time.

In the actual meeting, Helen only started to lose it once. She jammed her elbows against her chair, forced herself to breathe and brought herself back before the banker noticed. The meeting went smoothly and they worked out revisions with only minimal tension.

Any pre-learned tension may leave you open to flooding. A field rep realized he was fine in the office, but would start flooding in traffic on his way to appointments. Knowing this, he did isometrics and kept soothing classical tapes in the car. A medical technician noticed she was prone to flood after too much caffeine, which made her more likely to snap at patients. But typically before a tough day she'd brace herself with a double espresso—which was exactly the wrong thing to do.

Breaking the Cycle

Once flooding happens it's easy to get irrational and stay that way. Adrenaline is not easily broken down by the body, and if not dealt with it will stay in the system for hours.

This is chemistry as cliche: The president fights with his wife over breakfast, kicks the dog, comes to work, snarls at his secretary and throws a VP out of his office. Word spreads and the staff takes cover. A few hours later he starts to simmer down, and employees once again venture out in the halls like prairie dogs coming out after a scare.

When people are flooding they aren't particularly aware that they're acting like ogres. They're mostly aware of a terrible, crashing feeling inside them. They aren't aware of the damage they do. High levels of adrenaline are basically toxic, which isn't surprising. People feel poisoned. They lash out because they think someone must be to blame and because they have no other way to get relief. Once they find a better way they're likely to use it, if only because lashing out seldom works.

One couple had developed a chronic pattern of fighting about money. After a long day, Laura, the wife, walked in while Martin, her husband, was doing the bills. Laura forced a smile and said, "Hi, honey." Martin snarled, "Better watch your spending for the next 30 days."

Normally, the fight would have started that moment, but this time Laura put down her briefcase and calmly went in the kitchen. Surprised, Martin followed and found his wife bench-pressing the counter with all her might.

Never having seen his wife act like this before, Martin asked what she was doing. Laura was too upset to answer at first, and just kept pressing until she could feel the adrenaline start to clear. Then she asked her husband to give her an hour. Puzzled, he left.

Laura warmed up some leftovers and sat down to think of what to do. She could see they were flooding and she didn't want to do this any more. It was always the same fight and it wasn't going anywhere. After a while she went back to talk with Martin, and for the first time she was able to coherently make her case about how she wanted to be treated when she came home.

Also for the first time, Martin didn't counterattack; of all things, he agreed with her. He was even embarrassed at being so surly and finally asked why she wasn't yelling. Laura explained about flooding and how it was ruining their lives. They could talk about this like adults and ended up having one of the best evenings they'd had for quite a while.

Pre-Programmed for Flooding

On an everyday basis, the brain maintains a balance between alerting chemicals such as adrenaline and calming chemicals such as serotonin. These chemical groups rise and fall throughout the day: adrenaline levels rise during a tense meeting and fall during a quiet evening at home. Serotonin levels fall and rise in counterpoint.

Each person has an overall set point for these chemicals. Too much chaos, violence or stress early in life can leave adrenaline levels set too high. Once the set point is established, adrenaline levels tend to stay too high for life.

People who grew up in the middle of chaos, stress or violence can end up pre-programmed for flooding. The tough and savvy entrepreneur who grew up wild on the streets of Brooklyn may be like this. It doesn't mean that he can't control his temper or even that all his wild stories are true. It does mean that his set point for adrenaline may be too high, and this can affect his behavior here and now.

People pre-programmed for flooding often describe themselves this way: "I'm a perfectly reasonable human being; it's just that other people provoke me." There's actually a good deal of truth in this: they are fine most of the time, but they get provoked easily and once provoked, they overreact.

Howard put it this way: "I'm not an angry person, but if someone gets in my face, I'm right there. I go from zero to sixty in three seconds. There isn't any middle ground." He once had a supervisor yell at him for no good reason, so he followed the man into his office and slammed the door so hard the glass shattered.

People pre-programmed for flooding aren't lunatics out of control, even though they may feel that way themselves sometimes. However, they do need to watch themselves more carefully than the average soul. That impulse to overreact never quite goes away, but it does get more manageable once you know how to work with it.

Long-Term Flooding

Prolonged, chronic flooding has particularly bad effects. People who live with chronic flooding may become vindictive, bitter and filled with bleak despair.

Long-term, chronic flooding even alters memory in the brain. Scientists who studied the effects in embittered couples found that people who lived with chronic, long-term overloads had lost the memories of their good times together. They could only remember the bad; good memories had disappeared.

For instance, some bitter couples couldn't remember where they went on their first date. Now, the first date must have gone well, at least well enough to have a second date. But they couldn't remember where they went or what they did. Yet the bad times they could remember vividly.

You've seen this change in people around you. Karen is about to divorce Roger. She says, "I never loved him. I was just kidding myself all along." Yet you can remember when they got engaged and Karen was crazy about the guy. Karen isn't lying to you now—she literally can't remember feeling love for Roger. Those memories are gone and they may not come back.

A similar effect appears in politics or on the job. Life is seen through a grim, hostile filter. Good things don't count; only bad things do, and good things are made to look bad: "Sure Jack liked my report. Watch, I bet he'll try to steal it." Good will gestures are seen as a trap; a pleasant "Good morning" is written off as a ploy. Naturally, this becomes self-fulfilling; other people stop making offers when they get only hostility in return.

Some people develop revenge fantasies, playing them over and over in their minds, fueling a blood feud. This is not merely sick human nature but the long-term effects of adrenaline poisoning.

You may have no idea how to deal with such people; they seem invulnerable to reason. You can list ten different ways others have tried to reach out to them, and these people will discount every one. Then they'll attack you for even bringing it up.

These people are acting from adrenaline poisoning. You may remember when this was a bright, cooperative human being. If you tried to describe them that way now, probably no one would believe you.

People trapped in obsessive flooding are rarely swayed by compromise or appeals to be nice. They don't feel nice and they feel no obligation to be pleasant to people they loathe. They don't want to control their anger; they feel other people deserve it.

Don't try to talk about flooding as anger control: talk about flooding as pain control. These people feel poisoned. If you offer it as pain relief, they just might try it. This is valid: they'll hurt less and they'll be better able to keep other people from jerking their chain. Flood control can bring a desperately needed feeling of self-protection and self-control.

Certainly don't argue with people who are in this state. It only raises their adrenaline levels which clearly does no good. Instead, be practical about it. Compare flooding symptoms and talk about getting relief from breathing or work-outs; you could even show them this chapter. But don't argue with someone who's already overloaded and who can't hear you anyway.

Once people start to control flooding for any reason whatever, their overall hostility is likely to drop. This isn't surprising, since they won't hurt as much and they won't be operating on raw nerves. They may have a long way to go, but this isn't a bad place to start.

Extreme flooding cases sometimes feel as if they must lash out, as if their bodies will kill them if they don't erupt, like their heads will explode or their hearts will crash out of their chests. Well, it won't happen. It's just a feeling. It's a bad feeling, but it's only a feeling just the same.

Sometimes you may feel adrenaline physically hit you like a wave. Don't let it throw you; work with that feeling. Feel the impact as it hits and feel it wash over you. It's like taking a breaker at the shore, but remember: the wave is not you. It's something that's slammed into you, but it's not you. You are something else.

Don't expect an instant cure for people with long-term flooding. It took years of flooding to get them this way, and it will take some time to change it. People will need to experiment with different combinations to see what works best for them. However, chronic cases are often willing to work on the problem, if only because they hurt so much.

Sudden Clarity

Under intense flooding, there may come a time when you suddenly hit a clear-headed calm even though your heart is pounding. You see how dishonest, low and despicable the other person really is, and that compromise is an empty charade. You form the slashing response that this person so richly deserves.

Shut your mouth and go outside.

At this level of stress, your mind can play tricks on you, like a drug-induced high. People used to down drugs and think they'd discovered the secret of life. They'd write brilliant, vivid poetry, and when they read it sober it was drivel.

When stress gives way to sudden clarity it just may be a chemical trick. You look at your boss in the heat of battle and suddenly think: "Yes! I should quit! Why didn't I see it before?" The reason you didn't see it before is because it's an incredibly stupid idea. It's only adrenaline that makes it seem right.

Once people make these wild decisions, they often stick to them because the idea once seemed so right. They may not remember *why* it made sense, but they think that anything that felt so right must have something going for it.

If it's really a good decision it will still seem that way three days later. Wait it out. You might avoid a mistake you could deeply regret.

Happy Smashing

Self-restraint may be excellent, but ultimately something needs to be done with fury. You may, after all, have a perfectly good reason to be angry, even though you'd rather not ruin your life over it. You can't just wish the feeling away. If you pack it down inside it will only come out later in a more explosive form.

One approach is to let the fury out—just not on living creatures. Smash things, not people. There'll be fewer regrets and your body won't know the difference. Don't punch walls, since walls have a wicked way of hiding brickwork and other nasty surprises. Leave walls alone and smash things you can see.

Recycling centers are excellent for this. You'll find thousands of bottles that will only get fed into a crusher later. Smash what's there or bring your own supply. The sound effects alone are worth it.

If you have no access to broken glass or don't care for the noise (no accounting for taste), try smashing old furniture. Any junky piece will do, the heavier the better. The best pieces need a sledge hammer or a crow bar. If your neighbors ask, explain that it needs to fit into the trash can, so you have to break it into small, small pieces. They may just come over to help.

What to Remember

Flooding happens to everyone. It happens in different ways, with different styles, but no one is immune to it. We're hard wired for this. When it hits—when, not if—you have got to be prepared to bring yourself out. Only then do you have any chance of getting back to problem-solving and a sane, functioning life.

TO CONTROL FLOODING IN YOURSELF

- **Watch for physical symptoms first:** pounding head, racing heart, short breath, sweaty palms, dry mouth. Make a list of your personal signs. Check the list when you're under stress. Checking the list is more important than yelling at someone.

- **Watch for mental symptoms:** jumbled thoughts, rotary thinking, or an inability to see options, do sequence or handle math. Also watch for sudden inarticulation, disjointed speech or suggestibility.

- **Use large muscles:** Go for a walk. Close the door and do jumping jacks or swing your arms in windmills. Use isometrics if you're stuck in a meeting.

- **Reverse symptoms:** If your breathing goes short, breathe deep and slow. If your fists are clenched, open your hands and stretch your fingers.

- **Focus on specifics:** List facts and read them back to keep your mind focused. Slow the pace.

- **If you can't break free of flooding at the time:** Recognize that you can't think and stop arguing. State clearly that you'd like to talk later, then leave and re-group. Try again after you have repeated the earlier steps.

- **Prepare in advance:** If a tough situation is approaching, practice putting yourself into flooding and taking yourself out again. You mind learned flooding; it can unlearn it. You can develop a resistance to flodding or train yourself to snap out of it.

- **Get it out of your system:** Go smash something, just not people or living things.

TO HANDLE FLOODING IN OTHERS

- **Watch for symptoms,** such as flushed face, pulsing veins, or disjointed sentences.

- **Don't talk at them** since they can't hear you. Instead, let them talk; give them time to vent. Ask sequence questions: What happened first? What happened next? Use a low, calm tone of voice.

- **Don't crowd them**, don't touch them and don't make fast movements. If they want to leave, let them.

- **Be prepared for thinking problems.** Don't demand math from someone who is flooding, and don't give complicated directions. Keep it simple, or wait until they calm down.

- **Avoid jargon.** Use short, clear sentences.

- **With chronic cases talk pain control,** not anger control. High levels of adrenaline are toxic; this isn't a comfortable feeling. But the process will take time. They didn't learn flooding in a day, and they won't unlearn in a day.

- **Work on yourself first.** Flooding is contagious, but so is calm. You can't hope to stop someone else's flooding unless you can stop your own.

Chapter Two

The Conflict Continuum

Now that you know how to keep your brain from unraveling in a conflict, it's time to step back and take in the rest of the picture. Certainly strange things happen that flooding can't explain.

But perhaps our understanding of conflict is wrong. There really isn't a single package we can safely call 'conflict.' Instead, there are different kinds of conflict that operate by different rules.

This why good-hearted, sensible efforts so often fail to work. It isn't that you didn't try hard enough, or that good-hearted efforts are hopelessly naive. It's that types of conflict are so different that different solutions apply.

If you pour water on a wood fire, it goes out. If you pour water on an electrical fire, it spreads. There's nothing naive or ineffectual about water, it just doesn't work on certain kinds of fires.

This chapter will cover the three most common types of conflict: problem-solving, power plays and blind behavior. These conflicts range along a continuum. Problem-solving is level one and often not very difficult. Power plays or psychological warfare are level two and much more trying. Blind behavior is level three and absolutely toxic. Between them they present very different kinds of problems and respond to different kinds of solutions.

But see for yourself. The next two pages show the conflict continuum. Look it over and think of different conflicts that have come up in your life.

Conflict

Normal Range
Movement up and down continuum

FIRST-DEGREE CONFLICT	SECOND-DEGREE CONFLICT
Problem-Solving	**Power Plays/ Psychological Warfare**
Conflict on Solid Ground	*Conflict as Morass*
HEALTHY	**UNHEALTHY**

Characteristics:	Characteristics:
1. Rational	Seemingly irrational, senseless
2. Exercises self-control	Lack of control; overkill
3. Appropriate behavior	Inappropriate behavior
4. Reasonable grasp of reality	Difficulties with reality; denial
5. Appropriate boundaries	Invasion of boundaries
6. Concerned with facts, information	Withholds facts, information
7. Stable; may be boring	False charm, flattery
8. Prefers a clean fight; able to negotiate	Accusation, manipulation, or whining
9. Flexibility	Rigidity
10. Self-esteem depends on own behavior	Self-esteem depends on superiority; belittling
11. Pursues an end to conflict	Conflict endless; re-ignites
12. Relatively stoic	Self-pity
13. Myopic towards other systems	Deaf to input
14. Finds second-degree behavior stressful, painful and degrading.	Crazy-making; crazyland starts here

Characteristics:	Characteristics:
"This is a problem. I need XYZ to happen."	"You stupid S.O.B..."
"How can we work this out?"	"You're so mean to me."
"Oh—I didn't know that."	"Trust me. Just trust me."

Underlying message:	Underlying message:
"I want to work this out."	"I'm good. You're no good."

Continuum

Increasingly Abnormal Range
Conflict stuck in a downward spiral

THIRD-DEGREE CONFLICT
Blind Behavior .... *Advanced:* Tyranny or Predation

Conflict as Quicksand

DYSFUNCTIONAL	PREDATORY
Characteristics:	**Characteristics:**
1. Blind to own behavior .... Malice, vengeful harm	
2. Increased overkill .... Rage seizures	
3. Power without checks or balances; .... Felonies	
No meaningful limits on behavior	
4. Believes own lies .... Forces others to lie for him or her	
5. Missing boundaries .... Collapse of boundaries	
6. Isolation; elaborate secrets .... Bell Jar effect	
7. Highly charming/convincing .... Jekyll & Hyde behavior	
8. High accusation, high manipulation; .... Abuse/ charm baiting the trap;	
low, but still existing ability to negotiate hostage negotiation	

All abuse systems:

Racism/sexism/religious prejudice .... Entrenched hatred/ blood feuds

Active addictions .... Late-stage addiction

Emotional abuse .... Sexual abuse

Warning signs may appear in victims first:

Numb or even participatory behavior

Failure to act in own interest

Tendency to react in extremes: remarkably passive or remarkably hostile

Characteristic statements (from observers):

"But he/she is such a nice person. You must be lying/ crazy/ evil."

Examples:

Overindulged celebrities .... Celebrity as predator

Absolute rulers (includes abusive managers) .... Toxic management/toxic mate

Addicts, alcoholics, workaholics, etc...................... The drug itself as predator

The most commonplace conflicts are problem-solving, or level one, and power plays, or level two. We'll look at those first before going on to the tougher cases that arise with blind behavior or predation. Problem-solving conflict has the stable feel of reasonable people dealing with life. It's hard, it's trying, but you're going to go on. A sane organization has a tough goal, so people do what they can to get it done. Two sane parents love their kids, so they do what it takes to get them to eat their vegetables and do their homework. There's pressure, there's scrapping, but by and large things work out.

People behave pretty sanely at level one. The goals get reached, the homework gets done and the broccoli gets eaten (more or less). Some of the broccoli gets fed to the dog and some of the homework goes in late, but enough things go right so that life goes on and doesn't hit stalemate twice every bedtime.

Power plays are a different creation. At level two, your kid may like broccoli but won't eat it just to show you. Your organization's goals may be reachable, but in-fighting and manipulation make the simplest tasks into a monumental struggle.

Level one conflict is the realm of fair fighting, good sportsmanship and honest rivalry. Problem-solving is fairly straightforward; people put in the work without a lot of angst and drama. When turmoil does appear, people try to get through it without bearing a grudge. Level one conflict is not bad stuff, and when it all plays out both sides may be better for it. Whether you got your way or not, you find you can live with the other side, and may find that you respect them and grew from the experience.

Level two conflict is altogether different. Power struggles last longer, spread more easily, and cost much more in time, patience and human collateral. Power plays are much more costly because there's much more resting on the outcome. Level one is just about broccoli, just about goals, so what you see is what you get. But level two carries a hidden agenda. The fight officially may be about broccoli, but it's really much more about one-upmanship. Homework becomes a battle of wills with all the parental chips on the table. Those kinds of stakes mean a much fiercer fight, which inevitably goes into psychological warfare. Once people get caught up in power plays, problems and solutions get lost in the drama. The boss *must* be right, that kid *will* do his homework. And whether these conflicts play out between unions and management, teachers and students, or husband and wife, there will be winners and losers. In turn, the losers lie in wait to get even next time. At level two the conflict is never over: the fight will re-ignite.

These two forms of conflict have a very different feel. A problem-solving conflict has a solid feel, like you have your feet on solid ground. A power struggle feels more like a morass; accomplishing the smallest thing is like crossing the Great Murky Swamp. With psychological warfare everything feels harder than it needs to be, which is the case.

Behavior and Boundaries: Appropriate vs. Inappropriate

At level one, people do some unexciting things. At work, they work; in games, they play. Playing first base, they don't coach the pitcher and when cheering in the stands they don't throw beer at the umpire. They stop at stop lights, pay their bills and generally get on with their lives. They deal fairly well with rules—any rules— as long as the rules make sense.

Appropriate words such as "please" and "thank you," are not unknown in problem-solving conflict. Appropriate boundaries are commonplace: privacy is respected, conversations aren't monopolized, and people talk on the phone without wondering who's listening or how it might be used against them.

Level one conflict also involves appropriate behavior: people feel comfortable enough to speak and listen, exchange ideas and manage different points of view even when they don't necessarily agree. There's a feeling that there's room enough for everyone, or at least all who play fair. Actions and reactions are proportionate, if not low-key. There's an overall effort towards seeing that everyone makes it through in one piece.

Often there's an actual joy in the push and pull. At level one conflict can be a contest, a contact sport like football; yet people can be having a good time. In a tough real estate negotiation, the rental agent called to eagerly say, "Yeah, she really lit into me, but I was ready for her. All right! Now, next time..." It's rough, they're knocking each other around, but they're having a good time and no one gets hurt. It's not a problem; they're doing fine.

Power plays are more erratic and rife with thrills and chills. Boundaries get strange and appropriate behavior goes missing. At work people may do their own jobs, other people's jobs, or no job at all. On teams you never know when they'll drop their position to tell a perfect stranger what to do. In business, employees may be treated as children, colleagues as rivals and clients as prey.

At level two, ordinary standards don't hold. A nine o'clock meeting may start at ten because key employees didn't bother to show, or it may get derailed by people chatting away while blithely ignoring the rest of the room.

With psychological warfare, people often want things they're not entitled to. If a door is closed, they'll want it open. If a file's confidential, they'll want it on their desk. If there's a concession the other side doesn't want to give, that's exactly the marker they can't do without. And once the prize is painfully relinquished, it may sit ignored for weeks.

Other kinds of boundaries go wrong at level two. A reprimand that should take place in private is held four-square in the middle of the office. Comments that would be in bad taste in a locker room are posted through the company email. Work consumes time at home, and personal problems consume life at work. If there's a limit, it'll be crossed.

I once helped rent an apartment for a 70-year-old widow. Her needs were simple: she wanted a tenant who would pay rent on time, not destroy the place and handle problems as problems, not as on-going personal crises (her last few tenants had been quite exciting). In short, she needed a tenant who did problem-solving.

I'd sent out a notice on some email lists and did the pre-screening for her. It was fascinating how people responded to the simple word "No." I might write, "No, the apartment isn't ready to be shown yet," "No, I can't make an exception for you," or "No, the landlady doesn't want her home number given out."

Some were civil, even gracious, on hearing that they had to wait. Others behaved as if "No" only applied to other people. Some took it as a signal that they were to throw themselves against me until I did whatever they wanted. I could see why the widow wasn't up for this.

Since this was all done by e-mail, I had only their words to evaluate them, which were enough. Did they know the meaning of appropriate behavior and could they manage appropriate boundaries? I turned over a short list of prospects.

Rational vs. Seemingly Senseless

Level one conflict has a rational feel; overall, it makes sense. You may not agree with the other side and you may wish they felt differently, but once you hear things from their point of view, you have to admit it makes sense.

Power plays often appear senseless; inexplicable things take place. Parents berate a teacher, knowing perfectly well their child is at fault. Negotiators walk out of a meeting, knowing perfectly well they're hurting their own clients. People shoot themselves in the foot, shoot a budding project, or shoot their marriage and leave it to die. The only thing that explains such incomprehensible behavior is that they intended to prove who was boss.

Level two conflict doesn't improve on close examination, while level three crosses into 'senseless' violence—people shot over parking spaces, pizza, or the TV remote. Yet no one ever argues that it was a particularly good pizza or a program worth dying for.

Actually, there is no such thing as senseless violence. It all makes sense, just not the kind of sense you'd hope for. It's not about the pizza; it's about power. A power struggle can erupt over pizza, blue socks or who gets to carve the turkey. The symbol doesn't matter; the power struggle drives the fight.

Concerned with Facts and Information vs. Withholds Facts and Information

Problem-solving conflict is reasonably good at dealing with reality. People can tell the difference between what is true and what they'd like to be true. They may prefer that they were always right or never deserved a reprimand, or that their own side never looked foolish. We would all prefer these things. However reluctantly, we learn to face facts, consider that perhaps we are wrong sometimes (though rarely! Very rarely!) and generally manage to carry on.

In contrast, psychological warfare does creative things with reality. Denial is standard. People flatly refuse to accept facts: bad reports, bad reviews, the suspicion of a bad marriage even as it crumbles around them. Facts are an enemy to be shouted down or stonily ignored. Of course this doesn't improve matters, but that is second to being Right.

Problem solving also works with information differently. People at level one like information; they're curious about it. They can be stopped in their tracks by a new fact, something unexpected they didn't know. Many times in mediation, one side will finally confess the reason for their actions and the other side will stop and stare.

"OK—the reason we canceled the job was because we lost the paperwork. All right? We screwed up. It was a stupid, amateurish thing to do, but that's what happened. So we blew the deadline and we didn't want to admit it, and that's how we ended up dropping the job. So shoot me."

This would stop the mediation cold. You could almost hear the other side changing gears: "What? You— what? Why— you never told me that. We could've straightened out the paperwork. Why didn't you tell me that?"

The action stopped cold when new information entered the room.

In level two conflict, nobody listens. New information can walk in, sit down and put its feet up on the table and no one will notice, and this isn't necessarily related to flooding. In power plays people can be just as bull-headed working from a dead calm. Psychological warfare becomes impervious to facts, nearly invulnerable.

A parent storms in to confront a teacher and the teacher pulls out the child's test scores. Do you think the parent will look at those scores? Of course not. That could prove she was wrong, so it's important for her *not* to look at test scores. Of course, it also means that her kid won't be improving, but that's not the point. A power struggle isn't about solving problems; it's about being Right.

In a problem-solving conflict information flows in a reasonable way. If there's something important for you to know, someone will tell you. If it's information you need for your job, you'll have some way of getting it.

With psychological warfare, people withhold information. This will be true even if they want to tell you, need to tell you and that information is crucial to get them what they want.

Take two divorced parents fighting over custody. They need to know each other's schedules so that they can switch off and deliver the kids. In a level one divorce, their schedules and vacations get passed along as soon as they're known. In a level two divorce, one parent will make the other jump through hoops to learn what the schedule really is and when they'll get to see the kids.

Now, these parents know they'll have to cough up the information eventually. They have to hand over the kids and they have to be sure the other one's around for it. Nonetheless, they'll withhold information and make their exes jump for it, time and time again.

Often people in power plays don't see this behavior as being unreasonable—they think they're just getting their own back.

One woman was annoyed with her co-workers and so refused to say "please" or "thank you." Her office became a remarkable place: whatever she asked for, she could not have. It was like a magic eightball, only whenever she shook it, the answer was "No." She couldn't have files, paperwork, office supplies or information on her own schedule. In return for this total lack of cooperation, she'd refuse to say "please" or "thank you." And so, whenever she asked for something...

Now, both sides had it within their power to stop this fight and neither side would do so. There was nothing difficult about it. The woman was told repeatedly that the staff wanted her to say "please" and "thank you." The staff was told repeatedly that the woman wanted her own materials so she could get her job done. Either side was perfectly capable of accomplishing this, with very little trouble involved. But neither side would do so, so the fight went on and on.

Pursues an End to Conflict vs. Conflict Re-Ignites

In level one conflict, people will do what they can to get the fight over. They find conflict uncomfortable and tiring, and they'd rather do something else. If there's a problem, they want it solved. In fact, they're apt to split the difference and rush a solution just to get it finished.

With power plays, nothing so sensible will happen. Even if you manage to solve the problem, the fight will start again. If people settle on the budget, they'll fight about time lines or the color of the furniture. It's much more like the daytime soaps—it just goes on and on.

Psychological warfare can stymie any attempt at lasting change. Line workers who have everything to gain by working with management will not be able to drop the adversarial stance. Managers who have become painfully aware that their sole salvation is to stop antagonizing unions will not be able to stop themselves from sneaking in one last "gotcha." At level two, people will fight the same fight even if it is futile, wildly inappropriate or ten years out of date.

Flexibility vs. Rigidity

People at level one are not necessarily flexible souls, but they have enough flexibility to solve a problem. If change is what's needed, they'll manage to change. They may not like change; they may look forward to change with all the enthusiasm of a trip to the dentist. Nonetheless, if trying something different is the only way to work with their kid or straighten out the office, then that, somehow, is what they'll do.

In contrast, people in power plays are rigid. They *won't* change, no matter what the cost, and they tend to see change as some kind of personal defeat. If their actions ruin the neighborhood or poison the office, then that's too bad, because they won't change.

People won't stop spending money, though there's nothing left to spend, or they won't stop picking fights though the obvious result is open ruin. They won't accept a new member of the family, or they won't forgive an old one for a trivial offence. If something changes without their permission—say, one of the kids discovers that she's gay—then that is taken as a personal challenge.

Take the senator who fully expects the nation to wait while he gets his morning coffee—and the right kind of coffee, in the right kind of cup. Or the CEO who faces a budget crisis by refusing to give up his private jet. It doesn't matter what's at stake. The ego becomes the vital interest, and everything else is expected to revolve around that.

Self-Control vs. Lack of Self-Control

With problem-solving, people show a characteristic restraint and self-control. They may start to lash out, stop mid-sentence, pull themselves together and start over again in a better tone. This isn't about being 'nice.' They are showing self-control not because they want to, but because it's the only way to get things done.

Peter Drucker tells about Robert E. Lee, who was furious when one of his generals acted out of turn and upset his plans, and this wasn't the first time this had happened. Lee was storming around in a rage, when one of his aides asked Lee if he was going to relieve the general of his command. Lee stopped and looked at the aide, amazed, and said, "What an absurd idea—he performs."

Someone may ache with the desire to once—just once—give this colleague a solid boot. She may vent in private, but when called on to act she'll hold herself back and do what's right, to the best of her judgment. If something harsh needs to be done, she'll do it, but she'll show restraint whether or not she wants to.

Level two conflict doesn't work like this. Psychological warfare is marked by a lack of self-control, a characteristic overkill. There's no sense of proportion. People draw blood even when there's no point and nothing to be gained by it.

In psychological warfare, rules of decency don't apply. You may look at a situation and wonder, "Was it really necessary to do this much damage?" That's a sign of a power struggle.

Negotiation
vs. Accusation, Manipulation and Whining

The most striking skill at level one is negotiation. Problem-solvers may have little education and no formal training in negotiation, yet have a perfectly sound grasp of the basic rules of give and take. They understand that to get something they give something, and they'll weigh and balance just how that should work. Negotiation seems to come naturally and it's often the tactic of choice.

In power struggles there's a sharp drop in the ability to negotiate. It's replaced one for one by entirely different skills: accusation, manipulation and whining.

Accusation includes insults, slurs and belittling behavior. A snub might be very 'polite,' but cruel. Sometimes the insult is subtle, no more than a pause, a turn of phrase or a tone of voice. Yet the message is clear: you are inferior.

Manipulation, in contrast, can be very pleasant: a little soft soap, some compliments and flattery, but it's still a power game. We all know people who are delightful but dishonest. They're charming, often attractive, hell on wheels with the opposite sex and not to be trusted for a nanosecond. Taking the advice that you catch more flies with honey, they set trap lines wherever life takes them. It's a smoother form of psychological warfare.

The last skill in psychological warfare is whining. Yes, whining is a skill set and a powerful position. In a gifted few it's practically an art form. These are the victim games that are used so adeptly in life and office politics.

Whining makes it possible to keep power without working, blame others for problems and even fend off jail if it comes to that. But whining can be a more subtle tool; it's often used to outwit other people, but more often used to outwit ourselves.

Whining is a way to get out of facing our own problems. Mate giving you a hard time? Whine about it. That will excuse hard drinking, casual affairs, or anything else you were going to do anyway. Owe someone an apology? Whine about it. Whine long enough, with enough bravado and pretty soon they'll apologize to *you*.

Victim games are useful, not only because they get us off the hook from doing difficult things, but also because they justify things that are otherwise impossible to justify.

Watch the timing when whining is in session. These people may sound helpless, even pitiful, but often the whiner is about to hit the offensive. They're about to lash out at the world they think has wronged them, or reach for something they aren't entitled to. Fairness doesn't count around whining. They need it, they want it. and they're ready to take it. You become an object in the way.

Consider these skills when compared to negotiation. Accusation, manipulation and whining are all ways to score points or get things without offering anything worthwhile in return.

Another way to look at this is the difference between fair fighting and dirty fighting. Fair fighting inevitably comes back to negotiation and communication. Dirty fighting depends on accusation, manipulation and whining.

There's another line of difficulty here. At level one, people prefer a clean fight and seem actively repelled by dirty fighting. This changes if they slide into level two themselves; then they're no longer quite so particular. But while in problem-solving mode, they'll be so put off by dirty fighting that they may refuse to engage at all, even when they're badly needed.

Eisenhower faced this dilemma with Joe McCarthy, who was actually past the range of this chart. McCarthy was a savagely dirty fighter and Eisenhower was one of the few people in the country in a position to stop to him. But Eisenhower wouldn't; he said, "I refuse to get down in the gutter with that guy." It was only when McCarthy turned on Eisenhower's beloved army that the president found a way to draw the line.

The point was not that Eisenhower should also become a dirty fighter—McCarthy was the master and no one was going to beat him at that. The point was to find a new approach, more effective than dirty fighting. That's what it took to finally stop McCarthy.

Self-Esteem from Own Behavior
vs. Self-Esteem from Superiority

People in problem-solving can manage appropriate behavior because they actually pay attention to what they're doing. They have certain standards of how they should behave and they try to live up to them. Sometimes they'll slip, sometimes sneak a shot in, but then they'll stop, pull themselves back and often apologize. They may not wish to stop, but they'll do it.

Level one conflict is often marked by a certain courtesy, like getting a ticket from a very good cop. The courtesy isn't because the cop likes you or because you've done something commendable. Courtesy is about the cop's own professionalism, a statement of who he is, along with the determination that no one will make him something less. His self-esteem is based on his own behavior.

At level two, self-esteem comes from being superior to someone else. People overlook their own behavior and may not have considered it closely for years. Their focus is on the other guy. They think George over there is pond scum and can list his failings in great detail. They know everything wrong with George; they hold the book on George and they're constantly flipping the pages.

Compared to a lowlife like George, none of their faults really matter. Were they short-tempered? George had it coming. Did they lie or cheat? Well, George would have done the same to them.

This is where the problem comes in. People become so focused on George they no longer think about what they're doing themselves, much less notice that their own behavior has gotten pretty rank. For people who don't like George, they often become someone very much like him.

Stoic, Often Boring vs. Self-Pity, False Drama

People in problem-solving mode are often oddly stoic. They don't do a lot of self-pity. I once handled a case with a young couple breaking up, where the woman, before she left, ran up her boyfriend's charge accounts. He took her to court to make her pay the bill.

It was quite a bit of money for him. We weren't able to work it out in mediation, so the case went back to court.

The judge looked over the facts, turned to the young man and said, "Love is blind and it's also expensive. This is going to cost you." He ordered each of them to pay half of the bill: her because she had run up the bills and him because he had handed over his credit cards.

This was not what the young man was hoping for, but he took the hit without blinking twice. He said "Yes, sir," and tried to think how he could make tuition. He flinched a little, but otherwise he took it head on.

Power plays, in contrast, are often steeped in self-pity. It may sound like bluster and bombast, but if you listen to the words it's actually self pity: "Look at the people who work around here. There's not one of them who wouldn't stab me in the back if I gave them half a chance. Not one of them."

That sounds very macho, but it's really self pity. Listen to people on talk radio. There's all the blood and thunder, but underneath it's self-pity. They feel very sorry for themselves and they want to make sure the rest of the world hears about it.

In level one conflict, people will describe a similar problem in rather blunted terms: "Not the most congenial people working around here. Don't know what's got into them." It's all rather understated: No drama, no bombast, no self-pity.

This odd understatement shows up in the most dramatic situations imaginable.

My mother once jumped between a black gang and a white gang just after a race riot and broke up the fight. It was the single bravest thing I'd ever seen in my short life. When I asked her about it many years later, she said, "I don't know. What was I supposed to do? Someone could have gotten hurt."

Soldiers who landed on D-Day would typically give the same kind of response: "I'm not a hero. The guys buried out there, they're the heroes."

Sima Samar was a female doctor in Afghanistan, who ran a chain of clinics and schools for women under the Taliban. While receiving an award she said, "The work I do actually is not very special, but the condition . . . in Afghanistan was very special. It was not easy. It was very difficult. They tried to put a lot of pressure on us, but we tried to find a way to continue the work we do." The reaction was muted and understated.

There's a downside to all this. People at level one don't climb on a soapbox and dramatize themselves, but they also may not pass on basic information so that others can learn from their experiences. The people we most need to hear from are often the ones who aren't talking.

This leads to another downside to problem-solving: these people are not only stable, they may be somewhat boring. It's not a bad kind of boring; it's the kind of boring of a sound employee or a good marriage, but it's undramatic just the same. They may not tell their stories at all unless specifically asked. Power plays, with their angst and drama, are much more likely to seize center stage. It may be cheap drama, but it makes better press.

That understatement found in problem-solving occasionally results in a dry sense of humor that's a welcome change from the usual bombast. One Chicago high-rise was having trouble with the neighborhood teenagers over a small private beach. Most of Chicago's lakefront is public land, but there are a few buildings that face directly on the water and so have tiny beaches to themselves. These small, secluded beaches are quite a draw for local teens.

As one resident put it, "They do what young people do on a beach at sunset. It's just that they're doing it in our front yard." That's a dry way of describing something that had to have been pretty exasperating.

Even when critical, people in problem-solving can show that dry, good-natured humor. One woman off-handedly described her sister's boyfriend as "just as worthless as two dead flies." Which only makes you wonder—was he less worthless than three dead flies? More worthless than one? Or are three dead flies enough to build something? If so, what? A dashboard ornament?

No one's going to be delighted at hearing that in the cosmic balance of things he's weighing in at two dead flies, especially if it's true. But it's hard to feel cut to the heart by it.

Balanced Sense of Self vs. Self-Righteousness

One of life's ironies is that often the people with the worst behavior have the best skills at justifying it.

People at level one tend not to justify bad behavior; they apologize and move on. Sometimes that means apologizing to people they detest, and the stoicism really comes into play.

In power plays, however, people get self-righteous. They're not only cruel but righteously cruel, as cruel as someone morally superior which allows them to be very cruel indeed. Perversely, that same self-righteousness prevents them from questioning their own behavior.

Self-righteousness is hardly the monopoly of the religious caste, although that's a standard case. Atheists get self-righteous, as do wife abusers or even drug dealers: "Hey, nobody makes you put this up your nose." It's the superiority that makes mistreating others A-OK.

If we're honest for a moment, we have to admit that we all get self-righteous at times. We claim the high ground and shove everyone else off. One of the most seductive aspects of level two is being Right, which would be great if it didn't do so much damage.

People at level one, on the other hand, seem to be less self-important. It's fine if they hold the high ground, but they don't see it as a monopoly or a birthright. 'Right' isn't something that belongs to them alone or a robe they wrap around their shoulders. Rather, right is something they pursue, work towards, try to find in tough terrain. Then again, sometimes 'right' belongs to somebody else.

This tolerance comes from a sense of fairness and proportion. Adults can laugh at how easy it was to be 'Right' as a teenager, and how hard it's been to be right ever since. People at level one have retained that hard-won piece of maturity: Right is not a foregone conclusion but a day-to-day effort, some days better than others. It's refreshingly human.

Characteristic Statements

In both forms of conflict, certain key phrases keep coming up. At level one, you often hear a kind of negotiation statement: "This is a problem. I need X to happen." They'll make their case for X, negotiate for X, explain why X is a good thing, and generally convince you of the benefits of X or why the problem needs to go away. They want you to do X, but they're talking as one adult to another.

Another characteristic statement that appears in problem-solving is "Oh. I didn't know that." It's the stop-action moment when new information enters the room. It's a pivotal moment and it shouldn't be ignored.

With psychological warfare, you hear entirely different kinds of statements that go with those three basic skills. First there's accusation: "You stupid S.O.B," etc., etc." Then there's whining: "You're so mean to me." Finally, comes manipulation: "Trust me. Just trust me."

This is not one adult talking to another; this is someone trying to get the upper hand.

Both levels also have underlying messages. At level one, the bottom line message is "I want to work this out." That why they're talking, why they're negotiating, why they're dealing with you at all. They may not know how to work things out, they may not even know why they're still trying; but it all boils down to they know there's a problem and they're trying to make something work.

In power struggles, the underlying message is entirely different: "I'm good, you're bad." It's not a lot more complicated than that. Sometimes there's "You'll be good if you do what I want," but that's followed by "Trust me. Just trust me." Don't.

Level Three: Blind Behavior

Level three conflict takes ordinary power struggles and carries them all a step further. An ordinary round of psychological warfare can shift back to problem-solving, if only to save itself. People go so far, then realize they'd better snap out of it if they hope to save the contract or get their kids to school on time. At level three, that doesn't happen. In spite of effort, treatment, and sometimes huge sums of money, people fail to get better. They're stuck in place in a steady downward spiral. Individuals or organizations dig themselves in deeper and deeper, caught in self-defeating loops and utterly ignoring solutions at hand.

Level three is home to the chronic, exhausting problems that seem to have no end: racism, sexism, active addictions, all the big social ills. The category also includes people who are simply so spoiled or powerful that their behavior bypassed normal limits a long time ago.

Blind behavior covers a broad range. It can be as commonplace as growing up to become your father (whom you did not like) or as extreme as becoming a career criminal. There's a high level and a low level. Low level blind behavior can be fairly quiet as things go to hell in a casual way. The high level results in forms of tyranny or preda-tion; it shows more raw malice and things go to hell with real intent.

For instance, Grandma may have Alzheimer's and be very sweet na-tured, but may also burn the house down by leaving the stove on at 3 o'clock in the morning. The family, which is trying feverishly to avoid putting her in a nursing home, may be kind and decent but will de-velop the exhausted, high-strung symptoms of classic co-dependence.

Another family may have reared a young sociopath who will also set fires at 3 AM. That family will also develop classic co-dependence, while trying to keep the kid from getting locked away.

One family has a malicious agent and one has a cheerful, friendly one, but the overall patterns are much the same, along with the likelihood of the house burning down. These patterns aren't triggered by simple malice. They're triggered by blind behavior.

What both styles have in common is that people can't begin to change their own behavior because they don't even see what it is. A three-year-old throws a tantrum not because he's a malevolent force but because he's not old enough to know any better. A paranoid schizophrenic acts out not because she's possessed by evil but because her brain is misfiring.

Now you might insist that some people, like Leona Helmsley, certainly ought to know better. And so they ought. But this isn't about what people *ought* to know but what they *do* know, and if you follow the aggrieved statements to the press by Helmsley you'll see a profound level of denial. She has so much power and is so used to having her way that she doesn't understand about these little people who keep getting underfoot and threatening her with jail.

Blind behavior also includes the IRS and other vast institutions, which have learned to abuse power not intentionally but because they always got away with it. As with monopolies, an organization that never listens and never has to listen becomes something deeply skewed.

The Quicksand Effect

At level two people get mired in power plays, but level three has the quicksand effect where the harder people struggle the faster they sink. The more the staff tried to explain to Helmsley that she couldn't act like that, the more angry she became and the more she took it out on them. Co-dependents do everything imaginable to reform the alcoholic, yet the family continues to deteriorate.

The odd part is the recurring pattern. The man who hated his last wife marries a new woman just like the first. The woman who hated her last job finds a new one, which she hates just as much in six months time. An organization may be killing itself from the inside and see itself on the brink of destruction and yet can't stop fighting.

Often people involved want desperately to do better, yet will fail repeatedly. The whole thing had me mystified. It was as if people hit an invisible wall that threw them back over and over. I could track the symptoms and map the behaviors but I couldn't see what they were hitting. Why would people fight viciously, hopelessly, with nothing to win and keep it up for years?

These were often intelligent, daring or ambitious people, yet they seemed to be thrashing in circles. What was it?

It was a long time before I finally noticed that people at level three were unable to see their own behavior. They could describe the flaws of other people in great detail, sometimes going back generations. Their view might be skewed but it was certainly thorough and sometimes could go on for hours. Yet they seemed to have little or no awareness of their own behavior. You might ask an abusive husband why he hit his wife and he'd reply, "I didn't hit her," then elaborate on what a whining bitch she was. Hitting her had vanished; it was as if he'd come equipped with an instant erase button. A co-dependent could describe the alcoholic's drinking, and the alcoholic could describe the co-dependent's nagging, but neither side seemed to have the smallest awareness of their own behavior. And without an awareness of their own behavior they had no ability to change.

You might think these people would be experts on their own behavior, having the inside dope, so to speak. You'd think they'd at least be interested in it. But they weren't—all their expertise was about somebody else, even if it was someone they hated.

This is what finally explained the strange patterns at level three: it wasn't ultimately about hatred or greed or despair, although those might be glaring symptoms. It was that people were blind to their own behavior.

An active alcoholic can lose his job, wreck his car, get his license revoked, have his wife and kids leave and see all these events as someone else's fault or perhaps as inexplicably bad luck. The moment he considers that he might have a drinking problem—and thinks this seriously enough to do something about it—marks the moment when his recovery starts. If he never gets that realization he's apt to kill himself before he stops drinking, while ruining other people's lives in the process.

People don't set out intentionally to destroy their children or demolish their careers. Arthur Anderson didn't intend to go bankrupt; management at Enron didn't intend to wipe out pension funds. People get preoccupied with pride or drugs or ambition, or sometimes nothing more than their own problems. Then, somehow, when they're not quite looking, everything goes to pieces. But let's examine just how it works.

Blindness

With blind behavior people can't get better because it's obvious they've done nothing wrong. In fact, it's clear the problem is you, because you're getting upset over nothing.

A manager had to fire an employee. The man's absenteeism was highest in the division, his project was over budget and none of his assignments had ever been completed. He'd already had two written warnings. The manager called him into her office, listed the problems and explained he would have to be let go. He leaned closer to her and gently murmured, "Why don't you tell me what this is really all about?"

The manager blinked a few times, then went down the list again and explained that he was being terminated. He smiled knowingly and said. "I know you have to tell me that, but what's really going on?"

Nothing the manager said ever got through. Worse, she couldn't get him out of her office. As a last resort, *she* had to leave and he was still working on her in the elevator. Despite the dazzling charm, the manager had the unmistakable feeling that if she said one wrong word she'd be in for a lawsuit.

There's a marvelous egocentricity at level three. You throw an exasperated fit because Pete's division is back in the red. Pete calls you a heartless bastard who always hated him anyway. You obviously believe the topic is cash flow. Pete obviously believes the topic is Pete. Naturally Pete doesn't move to fix the cash flow, because he knows the real issue is just that you hate him.

You explain on a scale of importance from one to ten, cash flow comes in at nine and three quarters and Pete would be lucky at two and a half. Pete responds, "See! You don't care a thing about me."

Galileo proved the sun didn't revolve around the earth. Nobody believed him.

Believes Own Lies

Denial first shows up on the chart at level two, along with reality problems, but by the time we get to level three the denial is much worse. People lie and believe their own lies. When Pete makes his case as a stellar employee, he believes every word that he says. When the abuser says, "I didn't hit her," he really means what he says. You can begin to doubt your own reality because they clearly don't doubt theirs.

One of the problems of blind behavior is this disconcerting sincerity. They're not lying in the usual way; they truly believe what they say, even when it's obviously untrue. In fact, you'll find, in making their case, these people are far more convincing than you are. You'd better have the facts at hand. They may never respond to the facts, but others will respond to solid evidence.

Overkill/Rage Seizures

By level two conflict, self-restraint gives way to fits of temper and overkill. By three the overkill gets worse, and by the upper end of three you can actually see rage seizures.

A rage seizure is an explosion of fury just short of an epileptic fit. Road rage qualifies, along with the foaming frenzy when Aunt Sylvia talks about her ex.

The mention of race in the wrong circles can set off a rage seizure. The same thing can happen with Israelis talking about Palestinians, Palestinians talking about Israelis, Protestant or Catholic Irish talking about each other, or any of them talking about gay people. A few years ago during an open meeting on gays in the military, people stood up before the microphones and speaker after speaker went into hyperventilating rage seizures, in public, on a podium, in front of perfect strangers.

Sheer prestige and arrogance can also result in rage seizures. One would think that having unlimited power might make people happy or somewhat content. Instead it often makes them spoiled and volatile.

Celebrities fall prey to this. Why would someone with millions of dollars and the world at their feet want to set fire to his hotel room? Why would sports heroes with the best of everything and every need fulfilled have such a propensity for smashing their girlfriends?

The ancients described this as hubris. The king, the hero, the nobility, (the rock star, the basketball player, the children of billionaires) the man who had everything and the worship of the world, began to wonder if he wasn't a god. And when he was displeased, god-like, he'd smash everything in sight. What is needed are normal limits to bring him back to earth.

Collapse of Boundaries

People with active addictions or vast amounts of privilege essentially have no limits. It's time to stop drinking; they don't. Warned that they'll be thrown out of school if they get caught with drugs again, they go on doing dope and throw their effort into not getting caught. If their driver's license gets revoked, they're soon back on the road and drunk again. If they know good lawyers or their parents are well connected, they can keep this up for years.

Sexual abuse or incest is a wholesale collapse of limits. Clergy covering for child molesters is a broad-based collapse of boundaries.

Batterers, when served with a peace bond, may immediately go and violate the bond even if they have to skip work to do it. If the peace bond specifies that they come no closer than a hundred feet, they will settle in at ninety. If that doesn't bother the object of their attentions, they'll come in to eighty or fifty, then disappear before the police arrive. When the police go, they're back.

Violence between adults is a collapse of normal boundaries. It's different with kids; kids are less developed than adults and may maul each other like little puppies. Adults mauling each other is a different story. Even officially sanctioned mauling, like organized boxing, shows a collapse of limits when a boxer, say, takes a bite out of his opponent's ear.

In fact, one of the indicators of level three is that behavior is so far outside the limits that it takes paid professionals to run normal life. Someone is always getting called in: police, lawyers, emergency room technicians, social workers, parole officers, psychologists, bankruptcy attorneys, U.N. peacekeepers, someone. People can't safely run their own lives, so trained professionals are required to intervene.

No Checks and Balances

To stay on track, we all need checks and balances. A nation without checks and balances becomes a dictatorship. A company without checks and balances becomes Enron.

As the saying goes, power corrupts and absolute power corrupts absolutely. This is why monopolies become so callous and why highly educated medical doctors can become so crude. There's no one to call them on their behavior.

A woman had broken her leg, a wicked spiral break that had to be set twice to get it right. After it was done the doctor asked, with a smirk, if she'd like something for the pain.

No professional would be so cruel without the absolute belief that they would never be called to account for it. No professor who harasses his students, no social worker who humiliates her clients would ever behave this way without complete confidence that they are professionally immune.

Members of large bureaucracies develop this heart-stopping callousness, if only because no one holds them accountable. People with great wealth and privilege can develop the same tendencies. Even the deeply religious succumb. One minister pointed out that giving a fundamentalist husband absolute power over his family was hardly going to encourage Christ-like behavior.

Without checks and balances people no longer notice that what they have done is wrong, or even unusual. If other doctors behave this way, and other social workers talk about their clients as scum, there is no reason to question their own actions.

Jekyll & Hyde Behavior

While level three is often more charming and persuasive than mere everyday psychological warfare, the extremes of this category can deteriorate into Jekyll and Hyde behavior.

Thomas Jefferson noticed that slave owners, who might be cultured, well-educated, civilized human beings, were subject to fits of uncontrollable rage. He saw it as a disease peculiar to slave-holders.

The extremes of abuse—and charm covering that abuse—can result in a profound split in behavior. Active addicts become one person sober and someone else drinking; predatory celebrities become one person in public and someone else in private. Abusive families have one face for the world and another at home. Enron had one corporate culture internally and another to show to the stockholders.

The Strange Case of Dr. Jekyll and Mister Hyde was, in fact, written about life at level three. A Victorian gentleman could do anything to the poor, feed any kind of vice, and still maintain a prim respectability. And since he could get away with anything with no consequences he eventually turned into something monstrous.

Both these faces are in some ways real. For instance, Selma in the fifties was a warm, caring place if you were white, and a harsh, dangerous place if you were black. Both were true; neither one was an illusion.

The civil rights marchers forced Selma to change by conjuring Mr. Hyde out of the shadows and putting him on public display. This forced the white community to the negotiation table, a feat which had appeared to be impossible.

High Accusation and Manipulation/ Hidden Ability to Negotiate

With blind behavior you can expect very high rates of accusation and manipulation, matched with a low, seemingly non-existent ability to negotiate. In fact, from the outside it appears this behavior is so self-serving and outrageous you'd think these people were incapable of negotiating at all.

Actually, people at level three can negotiate, you'd just never know it by the way they behave.

This was one of the secrets of the civil rights movement. From the outside, it looked like there was no talking with the white power structure of the South. To all effects and purposes, it looked like it would never change, that whites would never come to the bargaining table. But when confronted by wise tactics, they did, in fact, come to the table and manage to talk things out. It was an entirely unfamiliar experience for powerful whites to bargain with blacks as equals; whites were brought to that table kicking and screaming. But they did come, they did adjust and they did learn to negotiate.

Because this level is so extreme, it takes special techniques to bring such people to the bargaining table and make them negotiate in spite of themselves. In later chapters of this book we'll look at ways to make this happen.

Characteristic Statements

Blind behavior operates within masks; the lies are believable and the outward package usually looks very good. If people from the inside start to tell the truth, people on the outside often don't believe them. In fact, the problem must be the victims, because they must be making the whole thing up.

The typical statement of level three comes from the outsider, and speaks to the uncanny charm: "But s/he's such a nice person. You must be lying/evil/crazy." This was Clarence Thomas and Anita Hill, O.J. Simpson with his car endorsements, the priestly predators who were so delightful their congregations didn't want them moved. These were all charming people, as long as you met them in public.

Signs Appear First in Victims

Because blind behavior is so adept at wearing a mask, the first signs of trouble may not appear in abusers at all; instead it shows up in the victims.

Consider an abusive couple in divorce court. He controls the money and the bank accounts, so he walks in looking good: new suit, well-groomed, often with a new girlfriend in tow. The wife looks like a stammering wreck in mismatched clothes from the Salvation Army. She's worried sick about the kids, hasn't slept and is flooding so badly she can hardly think straight.

If the judge has to decide which one gets custody he can be greatly misled by appearances. Fortunately many judges are trained to look for this syndrome and double-check who has the arrest record.

Corporate looters look prosperous and dynamic, while whistle-blowers sound like they're making things up. The predatory priests looked far more respectable than the stammering kids who were trying to be heard.

Because the abuser looks so good, and the abused ones look so bad, victims often despair of telling the truth. They don't even try because they think no one will believe them. This perpetuates white collar crime or well-bred, well-spoken child abuse.

This leads to the strange isolation I call the bell jar effect. Abuse seems to happen in a world of its own, as if behind a glass wall. Even when help is clearly in sight, the victim fails to reach out for it. A child enduring incest can go to school every day around teachers, friends and counselors and never say a word for years. It's as if she's living within an invisible circle that can't be crossed. The same pattern appears with abused wives, corrupt companies or desperately mistreated employees.

Victims at level three also show an uncanny failure to act in their own interest. Persecuted employees become too depressed to leave, and simply shut down and take orders. The abused daughter tells no one. The co-dependent husband doesn't cut and run, but bails his addicted wife out of jail.

Finally, victims at level three often develop what seem to be inexplicably extreme behaviors. They may be strangely passive, even apathetic to their own fate, then abruptly lash out in murderous ways. An abused wife may endure years of mistreatment, lie to the police and bail her husband out of jail, and then stab him in his sleep one night. Between doormat and assassin there's a fair amount of space, but with blind behavior victims may veer from one extreme to the other, sometimes with very little warning.

At level three, normal survival skills don't happen. Instead abnormal survival skills appear: going internal or shutting down, abasement, rage, or gross compliance. Most of these skills play directly into the hands of the abuser, which only perpetuates the problem.

Trends

Now you have the full overview of the chart. There are actually more categories, both good and bad, but these are the ones you're apt to encounter in everyday life.

Certain trends appear as you move along the continuum. In first-degree problem-solving people are most independent and individual, with that spark of originality that comes when people are fully themselves. They tend to get more done and do it in a less costly manner, both financially and emotionally. They're more reliable and easier to work with; there's less soap opera and more content. These people may not be very dramatic, but when you examine what they do they're really very interesting.

Power plays are more dependent and less individual. Both sides are interlocked: rivals watch each other, worry about each other and often mimic each other. Like two opponents at tug-o-war, one can't move without moving the other. There's less of the feel of real life and more of the style of melodrama, and of course it goes on and on.

By level three, there's a yet greater loss of individuality. People lose the spark of individuality and become more like stereotypes: the stereotype of a bad boss, a yuppie hustler or a whining in-law. By the upper end of level three, the dysfunction starts to subsume the personality: one end-stage alcoholic is much like another, and tyrannical bosses are oddly alike. Over time they become less like the original person and more like a clinical disorder.

As people cross into unhealthy terrain there's also a loss in maturity. Problem-solving conflict shows the most maturity and self-control. Power plays show a distinct loss of the same. As you go further down the continuum to the deepest part of level three, you find frankly dangerous human beings who behave basically like children. Tyranny is childish. Egocentric celebrities are juvenile. These may be brilliant, talented people, but their behavior becomes increasingly infantile.

With all these different characteristics, please keep in mind that no category includes the word 'nice.' 'Nice' isn't really part of the system. After all, this is conflict and no one may be in a very good mood. But adults still control their moods and try not to inflict them on other people. So the benchmarks aren't about what seems nice. Charm and flattery feel wonderful, but they may mask patterns that are deeply unhealthy.

These benchmarks are important. If you don't know the signs of healthy behavior, you have no way of knowing when your own behavior is going wrong, when a conflict is heading for trouble, or even when the other side is trying to shift for the better. You may be waiting for the phone to ring some sunlit day, when you pick up the phone and your bitter rival says, "You know, you were right. I was a jerk. We should have done it all your way."

While you're waiting for this hell will freeze over, the national deficit will end, and you will miss the valid signs of a normal person trying to come to terms with you.

Tying it All Together

Now, you may look at all this and think, "I've got it, I know how this works. I'm at level one and everyone who annoys me is at levels two or three."

That's not how it works.

Everyone short of a Zen monk moves up and down this chart. Mother Teresa moved on this chart. Someone flooding is apt to move to level two, rife with irrational, rigid, inappropriate behavior. Someone living with chronic flooding, with its long-term bitterness and loss of happy memories, is apt to be at level three. These are human conditions. It's normal.

Aside from the hazards inherent in flooding, the more difficult parts of this continuum have the gravitational pull of Jupiter. You may start at level one; most of us do. But then with a little provocation—some sharp words and impatience—we do what's normal and veer to level two. And once there, we tend to stay. It's a downhill slope: it's easy going to power plays and a lot harder getting back. To make matters worse there's level three with the quicksand effect, where it's extraordinarily hard to get out at all.

The encouraging part is that problem-solving also has a gravitational pull. That is, if you hold your course, stay calm and steady, and refuse to give in to provocation or self-righteousness, you can pull the other side over to you.

Any parent knows this. If you let the kids provoke you, you can shout to your heart's content but you have abdicated your place as an adult. You're no longer in charge, they've pulled you off center. If you keep your head and insist on behaving like a grown-up, you will see them come over to you. They won't suddenly grow up or see things your way—they aren't grown-ups, they're kids and they have a different point of view. But they will come over to problem-solving—perhaps reluctantly and secretly grateful for it. You get to behave appropriately as the adult, and they get to behave appropriately as children. Life can go on.

It isn't just kids who are pulled back and forth. We all do it. If you are working with someone who does accusation and manipulation, you'll forget your good intentions and find yourself slipping to level two. Conversely, if you're working with someone sane and stable, you'll find yourself moving to level one. If you see them both on the same day, you can watch yourself by turns become irritable and rigid with one and sensible and flexible with the other.

For you to have a future, you need to keep from being dragged back and forth. You can't be thrown off course by other people who may not want what's best for you. Or be thrown, perhaps, by people who do want what's best but who temporarily have lousy judgment.

For you to have a future, you need to keep from being dragged back and forth. You can't be thrown off course by other people who may not want what's best for you. Or be thrown, perhaps, by people who do want what's best but who temporarily have lousy judgment.

What to Remember

- **Level one traits** include a solid feel, rational behavior, self-control, a decent grasp of reality with appropriate boundaries, an interest in facts and information, an underlying stability and a willingness to negotiate. In this range people tend to be relatively stoic and mindful of their own behavior.

- **Level two traits** include seemingly irrational behavior with a lack of control or overkill, denial and difficulties with reality, withholding information and false charm. Skills include accusation, manipulation and whining. There is also rigidity, self-pity, and self-esteem that depends on being superior to others. By level two, solutions get much harder and a conflict will re-ignite.

- **Level one conflict is less damaging** than level two and ultimately much more interesting.

- **Level three conflict** includes the chronic, crippling problems of the world: racism, sexism, homophobia, hatreds of all sorts, and grinding, seemingly unsolvable problems like active addictions, crime and endemic poverty.

- **Level three** is like level two, but more so: more overkill, more problems with reality, even more charm and manipulation. The big difference is that without self-awareness, people lose their capacity to get better. They can't readily move back to problem-solving; blind behavior becomes a long, slow downward spiral.

- **People become oblivious to their own behavior** by level three. A bigot really sees himself as fair-minded; an active addict really believes she can stop at any time; a thug really believes he's a hero. Discussion or facts have no particular effect on this.

- **Level two can shift** back to level one problem-solving, where conflicts are much easier to handle. Level three can't shift to a better place without a massive, shocking jolt, such as hitting bottom in the case of an active addict or threat of collapse in a family or company. You'll either have to jolt it or deal with it where it is.

- **Symptoms of Blind Behavior** include the quicksand effect, the collapse of normal standards, out of control power, people who believe their own lies, a low, but still existing ability to negotiate, and Jekyll and Hyde behavior.

- **Outside professionals** are regularly required at level three. Ordinary life involves cops, lawyers, social workers, emergency room technicians, spin doctors or peacekeepers.

- **Visible problems** are apt to appear first in the victims. Victim characteristics include a tendency to react in extremes, either remarkably passive or remarkably aggressive; numb or even participatory behavior, and a failure to act in their own interest. Victims are as trapped in blind behavior as anyone else.

Now that you can see how conflict works, we can start talking about what techniques work where. On the next page you can see how flooding fits into the system.

What Works Where

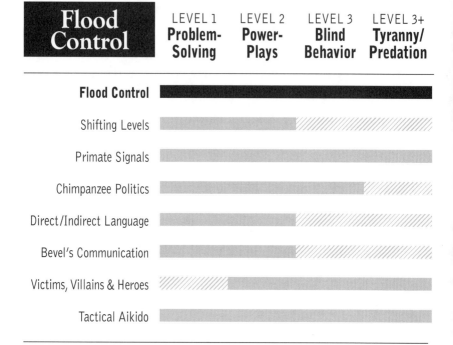

Flood Control	LEVEL 1 **Problem- Solving**	LEVEL 2 **Power- Plays**	LEVEL 3 **Blind Behavior**	LEVEL 3+ **Tyranny/ Predation**
Flood Control				
Shifting Levels				
Primate Signals				
Chimpanzee Politics				
Direct/Indirect Language				
Bevel's Communication				
Victims, Villains & Heroes				
Tactical Aikido				

Flood Control is crucial in any kind of conflict. Flooding will interfere with problem-solving, drive a conflict to psychological warfare and can become overwhelming once you reach the chronic patterns of long-term abuse.

Here also you can see the importance of concentrating on your own behavior. You may never succeed in getting a rageaholic to calm down; however, you are also apt to start flooding, so flood control will be crucial to your success.

Chapter Three

Shifting to Healthy Conflict

The first crucial conflict management skill is learning about flood control, since that's what's needed to keep a working brain. The next crucial skill is benchmarking where a conflict falls on the continuum. Once you understand what type of conflict you're facing, you'll have a better idea of what to watch for and what you might do. Since different techniques work with different levels, it's crucial to know where things fall.

We'll start with techniques for level two power struggles, which are the most common, everyday conflicts. Since blind behavior is much more difficult, we'll focus on that later in the book.

Remember, in the first two levels people readily shift back and forth. And since people move so easily at this point, one of the best things to do is to encourage them to shift for the better. One way to do this is to plant yourself firmly at problem-solving and pivot the others back towards you. This can be done even when the situation is spinning out of control.

During a downsizing a team of managers were instructed to decide who to cut. One quarter of the staff would have to go. The CEO asked a senior manager, Eliot, to chair the meeting.

The first round of discussions was painful but basically sane and fair. Facts were on the table and the discussion was mature. It was first-degree problem-solving. It was only after the managers realized that they could not meet their numbers by the easy cuts that the process abruptly got ugly.

Managers started attacking each other's staff, dredging up dirt and covering for their own. When Eliot tried to intervene they quickly turned on him. Now Eliot felt insulted, outraged and aggrieved; the meeting was disintegrating into a shark-fest. Then Eliot heard the sound of his own voice and realized he was simultaneously attacking and whining: he had followed the others to level two.

This snapped him out of it. Even as the others were battling, he remembered there was a reason the CEO had chosen him to be in charge, and he took his place as leader.

Eliot stopped the meeting. He informed them all they were letting things get out of hand and the company expected more from them than this. If they lost their heads then everyone else would, too, and they couldn't afford it.

He gave everyone ten minutes to cool down, and then they were to come back and put all the facts on the table. There would be no more withholding information and no more personal attacks. They would open all personnel files and review performance ratings for the last two years. They were going to handle this in a responsible manner because the rest of the company was counting on them to do so.

The other managers snapped out of it. The rest of the meeting still wasn't pleasant, but it was stable, fair and rational. Everyone lost staff they didn't want to lose but they handled it with decency. Once Eliot realized he had slid into the morass, he could get back to problem-solving and get the others out.

Gateways to Problem-solving

As I've said before, people aren't static on this chart. Everybody moves. On a good day, in a good mood, people live at problem-solving. On a bad day, when people are hurt or frightened or offended, people move to power plays. That's what humans do.

However, people move along some lines more easily than others. Some lines serve as gateways.

In the above case, Eliot called for three basic things: self-control, appropriate behavior and appropriate boundaries. Those are the easiest places to stop the slide. He set fair, decent standards and saw to it that everyone equally held to them. By gauging his own behavior, he could make others aware of their own behavior. Finally, he made them stop withholding information and deal with open facts.

If you think about it, this was not unlike the approach used by mediators. People don't come to mediation in the best of moods; they're often angry, threatened and enmeshed in power struggles. However, the mediator sets the tone by laying out clear rules and boundaries: there will be civil language, civil behavior, and both sides will take turns telling their stories.

This has a stabilizing effect. People want to interrupt, but they'll stop themselves. Annoyed as they are, they'll exercise self-control and watch their own behavior. They'll follow the rules, clean up their language and take turns, even with someone they don't like. Once they stabilize that far, the mediator can take them the next step: to be more open with information, more flexible and more realistic in their view of the problem.

The best gateways to problem-solving are those first invoked by mediators: self-control, appropriate behavior and appropriate boundaries. Once people begin those behaviors they can grow more flexible, shift back to negotiation as opposed to accusation or wheedling, and do less drama. In time they might stop withholding information and give up self-pity.

People shift on some traits last, if at all. For instance, at level two it can be very hard to get someone to face reality. You can take the furious mother confronting the teacher, tie her in a chair and force her to read her son's report card. It won't improve matters in the least. In a similar sense, it can be very hard for people to give up self-righteousness; it's just too great a temptation.

Once people move along any of these lines, you will see them move along the others. If you can get them to exercise self-control and watch their own behavior, you will also see them become more flexible, drop unfair fighting and go back to working on the problem. It's actually quite exciting.

Flexibility does not have a direct correlation to self-control. A grasp of reality has no direct link to stoicism or a lack of manipulation. Yet a change in one will result in a change in the other, so you may as well start with the easy lines first.

Getting Others to Change

This, of course, leads to the primary question: how do you get other people to change? Given the slippery slope, the everyday temptation of victim games and one-upmanship, how do you get other people to straighten up and fly right? How do you get them to alter their behavior so that they will be more reasonable and stop giving you such a hard time?

The answer is: You don't.

That's right. You leave them alone and focus on your own behavior.

Remember, just as psychological warfare pulls other people to a different level, so does skilled problem-solving. I won't lie to you: it's easier to move someone to bad behavior than it is to move someone to good. Any idiot can provoke bad behavior, while leadership is needed to improve things. But in that same sense, leadership means showing the way. If you calm down, you can get them to calm down. If you respect fair rules, others can learn to respect fair rules.

You can only lead by example. No one will do this if you won't do it first.

Now, you may balk at this: Why should I calm down? They're provoking me. Why should I be the one to change? Let them calm down and be nice to me!

There's a saying attributed to the Rev. James Bevel: "We keep expecting other people to be better than we are." And they're not. We expect them to listen to us, when we don't listen to them. We expect them to calm down when we don't calm down. People do not do this. If, by chance, it ever does happen consider it an act of God but don't expect it to happen again in your life.

To take charge of a situation you have to first take charge of yourself. To be a leader you have to control yourself before you can hope to have influence on anyone else. This will require all your attention, strength and wisdom. Other people will have to wait for enlightenment while you somehow wrestle your actions into line.

There's another saying attributed to Bevel: "No progress can be made as long as we defer responsibility." Our conflicts are not going to be solved by other people. No one is going to appear and improve our lives for us. Certainly people ought to act better; they ought to accommodate us. And we ought to win the lottery and live in a fine house with a view of the ocean. And as long as we're waiting for someone else to make these lovely things happen, nothing is going to get done. If solving problems really matters to us, we need to see to it ourselves.

Actually, working on yourself first is a good thing. Just like controlling your own flooding, it puts you in a position of strength. It also leaves a few billion other people to wait their turn while you handle exactly one. That's good, the odds are better. Meanwhile, what you learn from handling yourself will give you much of what you need to deal with everyone else. From watching yourself go through these changes, you will learn to move others through similar changes. You will also learn patience because you will learn, first hand, just how hard those changes are.

The Shift under Pressure

Now I have to tell a story on myself.

I had broken my collarbone, which is a wretched thing to do. The problem is that the break can't be cast and there's no way to take the weight off the bones. So if you make a wrong move the bones shift and grind, which is just as awful as it sounds.

To keep some pressure off, I had my right arm taped to my body, which gave me only my left arm. I was teaching at the time and had to drop by the library to do some copying. It was the first cold, wet day of the season and I discovered how much broken bones hurt with a change in the weather. I hadn't packed enough pain pills and worse, I was hauling a raincoat, umbrella, attache and books, all of which had to be balanced left-handed.

Naturally I'd drop things, and as I stooped to pick things up, the break would wrench. The worse the pain got, the more I dropped things, the more I wrenched the break, and so on. Then I discovered that the copy machine was on the far side of a massive door which couldn't be opened with one hand. Struggling with it, I dropped my papers, which wrenched the break, etc, etc.

I finally realized I was going to kill myself at that rate, so I ferried my belongings over to the library desk and explained the situation to the clerk working there. I asked if I could leave my things behind the desk while I took care of the copying.

He said no.

I could feel the top of my head lift off, like Vesuvius. My first thought was that I would kill him and drag his body up and down the length of the library. This struck me as reasonable. No jury would convict me.

Because of my head lifting off I had some suspicion I might be flooding, so I took a quick scan of what I needed to remember about level one behavior. I could picture the chart: it was completely blank except for the numbers. Struggling, I managed to remember the bottom-line statement of healthy conflict: "I want to work this out." So I took a deep breath and asked the clerk, "OK, then. What would you suggest?" I have no idea if the whole process took two seconds or five minutes. I was very civil; it was hard to get the words out. I expected the clerk to say something officious and then I could kill him and lay waste to the library.

The clerk thought a moment and replied, "Well, I could help you carry your things over to the copier. We're just not allowed to hold packages behind the desk."

Then this perfectly nice, courteous man scooped up my books and umbrella and walked with me to the copier. When he saw me struggle with the machine he lent a hand and on the way back he helped me get the books back in the rack.

I was dumbfounded. I had veered to the homicidal edge of the chart without ever noticing. Of course I was going to lay waste to the building, but I didn't think it was anything unreasonable. I felt beset, at my wit's end and thoroughly justified. The fact remained, I nearly tore into a perfectly nice soul who actually was willing to help me.

It was an unsettling experience, but it taught me a few things. Of course, when flooding I went to the wrong end of the chart, but it didn't *feel* like a power play at all. I was convinced I was justified.

There are plenty of excuses I could make for myself, all of which are irrelevant. What mattered was to be prepared for this. Years ago I drove a junker that veered to the left when I put on the brakes. Excuses didn't matter—I needed to know how that car would move. Understanding the veer kept me from hitting a pedestrian who walked out in front of me on an expressway.

Everybody veers under certain conditions. It may be when you feel thwarted, or when your authority is questioned, or when someone yells at your kids. The better you know yourself, the less that veer will be a danger to you and the more you'll be able to handle the forces in play.

It's also simple tactics. A key characteristic of level two conflict is that it can be shifted back to problem-solving. Since people can move back to health y behavior, the most forthright solution is to get them to do so. Once they're back at level one, they may well solve the problem themselves. But they're not going to do that unless you go first.

What Shifts?

I used to teach the continuum in negotiation class, since it basically governs the action. At level one, negotiation skills are strong and central. At level two negotiation skills give way to psychological warfare and the negotiation suffers accordingly. I could watch the negotiation stay on track or veer off course by watching people move from level one to two and back again.

I started asking students just what it took to shift them back and forth. These are some things they reported:

"I take the argument personally and respond personally. Usually when I say something that is not nice I get a strong feeling that I have hurt someone's feelings. I then realize it and instantly revert. "

"My voice gets higher, I talk faster, often repeating myself... I stopped listening. Returning, my voice slows down, I find myself breathing deeper and responding in a more clear, rational manner. Sometimes it was effective to have a teammate slip me a note that read 'Shut up.' This shocked me into returning to a calmer state."

"I began to get defensive as well as giving up flexibility; I started to resent and disbelieve the other side. I felt insulted. I returned after a good faith gesture."

"I began flooding; then I realized that I needed to get more information before I start jumping to conclusions."

"Using power and dirty tricks signals my move to level two. Thinking about the other party's needs signals my return to level one."

"When I felt insulted; felt I was losing control, I turned negative and resisted more. Returned to level one by taking a break; either stepping away or letting someone else negotiate."

"I become indignant and frustrated."

"When a member of my group would not acknowledge my input I moved to level two quickly. I became angry, flushed, with tensed body stance... I spoke sternly and curtly to our self-appointed leader.

"I regained my composure when my financial expertise was needed...

I took a deep breath, took a look at the bigger picture, and spoke up."
These people had learned how to tell when they were moving in and out of healthy behavior. What remained was how to guide it.

The Transition Zone

There's a space between levels one and two that's basically a transition zone. You haven't done anything inappropriate yet, but you easily could. You're lobbying your boss for a change in your vacation schedule and she's just said something that touched a nerve. You can feel your temper rise and the come-back right on the tip of your tongue. You're on your way and with a very little pressure you'll go over the edge, whether or not it costs you that weekend.

With my broken collarbone, pain and frustration took me to the transition zone. Of course I wasn't intentionally acting out, nor was anyone provoking me. In fact, during the transition I had no contact with any human being. I was provoked, but there was no one to provoke me; it was just me dropping books. Gravity and I were having it out and gravity was winning. But the first person to say a wrong word took me over the edge.

One thing I did right was to manage that transition zone. I hadn't acted out—yet. I might have been at the very edge, but I held it off for a moment and that moment turned out to be exactly what was needed. Because I caught myself and held that moment, I was able to do my copying and exit the library without having made an immortal fool of myself.

Working with this chart, after all, is not necessarily about having 'right' emotions. Emotions matter—they are prime, invisible driving factors. But this chart is really about behavior. You may feel furious and wildly unreasonable, but if you manage to get out something civil then you haven't yet blown things.

This is not the Catholic church. It's not an equivalent sin to think things that you don't actually do. Just not doing it is enough. A good deal of the time people in problem-solving mode don't want to be patient and sound. They're choking back words and keeping themselves from reaching over and throttling the other guy. That's self-restraint and an excellent step in the right direction.

Now, people don't slip into power struggles out of sheer bad nature (All right, some do, but not you or me). Instead, something triggered them. The more you know about triggers, the more you can keep them from mastering you.

Frustration/An Inability to Get What Is Needed in a Healthy Fashion

In the library I was in pain and I needed cooperation from a stranger. Having few working brain cells at the time, I believed I needed to start World War III to get it. Just how I would get cooperation by laying waste to the library was unclear, but this was my intention.

Sometimes people work themselves into a frenzy simply so they'll be taken seriously. One woman threw a fit at a hotel because she missed her wake-up call and wanted a refund. She was belittling and rigid and she lied through her teeth. She was embarrassed by the way she acted—and it was just an act—but she believed she'd never get her refund if she didn't act this way.

People who are angry are usually people in trouble, whether or not they're willing to admit it. Sometimes it's enough to stop and listen.

Active listening may have become a cliche, but it's a perfectly useful technique. It assumes that angry people say angry things, so you ignore that. You filter out the bad language and isolate the message, then repeat it back in your own words to see if you got it right. After a barrage you say: "You're mad about the delivery." Then you get another barrage because that wasn't exactly the point: "You're mad about the delivery and the attitude of the guy in the green uniform." As you keep filtering you get to the problem, which may be quite different from what you expected.

Respectful listening can stabilize things when, frankly, there is no solution. Mac was the emergency manager for a pharmaceutical line, who came back from the holidays to find a furious call from an elderly man who had had a bad reaction to a drug. This was a skin medication and about 10% of the population will react badly. There was no way of telling in advance who would get the reaction, and what was worse, once the tube was opened it couldn't be returned. And this stuff was expensive.

The patient was furious because no one was at the office over the holidays and the drug wasn't listed with his local poison control. He was OK by then, but he was threatening a lawsuit and an FDA investigation.

He had every right to be upset. Once Mac got a grip on all the problems that had gone wrong, he could do a few things about it. He could get the drug listed at poison control and he could set up a beeper system so in the future he could be reached over the holidays. However, he couldn't undo the painful reaction and he couldn't take back opened medication.

By the end, the customer not only accepted Mac's apology, he offered to be the company's local representative. Respectful listening gave him the chance to take control over the situation. The changes couldn't help him, but they would help the next person and that set things right by him. He was back at problem-solving and out of level two.

The calming powers of active listening seem somewhat odd, unless you think of the bottom line: these people aren't upset just because something went wrong, but also because they feel disrespected. To stop and pay attention to them is a way of showing respect.

People stop and listen to the president or the pope. People don't stop and listen to Sam the bus driver. It's not a treatment that many people get, and frankly we all could stand a little more of it. It's supply and demand: since respect is in such short supply, it creates a high demand.

Active listening is a good-faith gesture, and that can have value.

People can stand things going badly; that happens in life. What they won't stand is being snubbed or willfully jerked around.

Now, this same technique can be abused by parroting back without listening at all. In that case it's a brush-off, a case of disrespect. People aren't stupid; they can tell when they're being patronized. They won't calm down, they'll swing deeper into overkill and certainly won't start problem-solving.

Accusation

Accusations quickly drive a conflict into psychological warfare. One guy wasn't getting the cooperation he needed, so he sent out a waspish e-mail. At the next meeting one of his colleagues took him to task for being rude and inconsiderate. Well, he was out of line so he apologized, but she continued to light into him in front of their co-workers.

Now he was not only insulted, he wasn't being listened to. She kept criticizing him and he got hostile, if only because she kept accusing him of accusing her. This degenerated into "You said..." "No, I didn't." "Yes, you did..." and other adult, businesslike exchanges.

Well, this guy caught himself. He realized he was being rigid and accusing, and trying to beat her down with his words. He also realized this wasn't going anywhere.

He pulled himself together and got his flooding under control. Realizing that the woman he offended was stuck, he addressed the other members of the group. Perhaps she couldn't hear his apology, but the rest of them could. Meanwhile, they'd heard enough and were ready to move on.

He also made an immediate concession as a good-faith gesture. The rest of the group accepted that. His adversary still didn't get it, but that was OK because he'd now won over the rest of the team. He'd admitted he'd done something dumb, but he could now put it behind him and to go on to do better next time.

Boundaries Revisited

I had the pleasure of hearing a talk on boundaries by an Indiana woman who was an Employee Assistance Program counselor. EAP counselors mainly work with employees with addictions, so these are not easy problems.

Even while counselors are coping with clients, they're also fielding calls from parole officers, managers or family members, each of whom may be pushing a different agenda.

This counselor realized that in all her years of training she had never been taught how to set limits with these people, not even advice as simple as what is all right to say to whom. The wrong word to the wrong person can get the employee fired or jailed, which wasn't exactly therapeutic. In the midst of all the cross-fire, how could she find the responsible thing to do?

Her answer was setting boundaries, and she defined a boundary as either a legal or moral obligation. A boundary that wasn't either a legal or a moral obligation was probably not healthy and was apt to come around and bite you.

Now, people under pressure will set boundaries, though they may not make the wisest choice. For instance, not returning phone calls is a way of setting boundaries, as is isolating yourself or being too busy to sit down with your family. Saying nothing and keeping everyone at bay is, after all, a form of self-protection.

Withholding cooperation, withholding information or making endless excuses are all ways of setting boundaries and keeping other people back. But these probably aren't good choices, and they're forms of power plays.

Once this has started, the first person's survival tactics are bound to trigger someone else's frustration. The pattern is: boundary violations lead to vulnerability, which leads to boundary violations.

For example: A three-year-old feels needy, so she follows Mom around, whining. Mom's boundaries feel violated, so she ignores her.

The kid feels threatened, so to get attention she breaks something. They're triggering each other and they go into a power struggle.

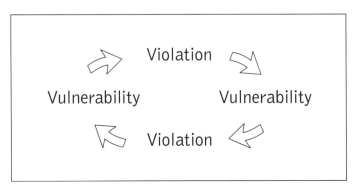

The pattern plays with a hundred variations. Alex is working too much, so he neglects the raking so that leaves blow into Betty's yard. Finally losing her patience, Betty rakes up the mess and dumps it back across the fence. So Alex shoves Betty's garbage container back across her property line, putting a hole in her shrubbery. "An eye for an eye and a tooth for a tooth" is very hard on gardens.

Violation creates vulnerability, which creates a new violation. This may have been intended for self-protection, but the pattern doesn't work that way. Note that the cycle doesn't read violation/ vulnerability/violation/*relief*. Relief isn't on this cycle. It just goes to a new violation.

But the Indiana speaker described a way out: find the legal or moral obligation and do that. That will set a boundary that isn't a violation and can hopefully stabilize the whole sorry mess.

Does Betty have a legal obligation to rake up Alex's leaves? Not without cash payment. A moral obligation to it? Not likely. But does she have a legal or moral obligation to dump the lot on Alex's roses? That's not true either.

So Betty spots herself in the transition zone, knows that she's feeling pushed, knows she's tempted to act out.... and then doesn't do it. She needs to set a reasonable boundary and set it with a skill from level one. There are a lot of possibilities: First control flooding. Go talk to Alex and be civil about it. Hire a kid jointly to rake up the leaves. Work out a deal with compost. But cross into psychological warfare and things will get abruptly get worse.

These are the same guidelines for moving back to level one: watch your own behavior. Choose from column A, not from column B.

The same rules hold if the cycle has lasted a lifetime. Sara was helping her father set up a convention booth, and they'd been fighting all her natural life. He'd tell her what to do, she'd resent it and they'd be at each other in a flash. Her father had always been hard to please, and quick to offer 'constructive' criticism which was actually belittling. Sara would defy him, they'd both start flooding and the fight would be off and running.

At the convention, Sara had to get hundreds of bottles of cosmetics sorted by style and color, and the bottles arrived in no particular order. Feeling overwhelmed and flooding, Sara started out in the transition zone.

Her father came over and looked at the mess, and told her he had a better way to do it. Immediately her demons kicked in ("See—You can't do anything right!"). Sara felt a wave of anger and self-pity. She cut him off before he could complete his sentence and insisted she was doing fine, which obviously wasn't true.

Her father asked her to just listen a moment—he had an idea that would make things easier for her. When Sara heard him say 'easier'—not 'better'—she forced herself to stop and listen.

Actually, her dad had a great idea. It seems the cosmetics were color-coded, so they took all the boxes and laid them out in columns by number. All the styles and colors fell into place, which made the job a snap.

Sara realized he was only trying to help, and she forced herself out of the transition zone and made herself stay flexible. She thanked him and told him this was a good idea. Her father was pleased that for once she actually listened to him. They both felt proud of how they handled it, which meant feeling self-esteem from their own behavior. It was a nice break from the power struggle that had lasted nearly thirty years.

Food

Sharing food is a powerful, deep-seated symbol of family and friendship. Friends willingly eat together; enemies do not. Breaking bread together is a symbol that appears in nearly every culture around the world.

Sharing food is such a deeply ingrained message that it's even used in hostage negotiation. For instance, when a gunman demands a sack of hamburgers the hostage negotiators never comply. Instead they send in deli food: some bread, beef, a little mustard, all the things to make a sandwich but never a ready-made meal.

The reason is that the hostage taker doesn't have time to put down the gun and make a sandwich—a hostage will have to do that for him. Psychologists have found that if a hostage prepares food and feeds the gunman, the gunman is far less likely to shoot the hostage. There's something bonding about handling food and eating together.

It's possible to tap into the same reservoir of good will in far less loaded situations. Sharing food is more effective if it's informal; you want casual, messy, down-to-earth food. One organization had its managers throw a company barbeque every summer, standing over the grills, painting on the sauce and serving up the food on big platters for all. It was great for morale.

This is not the time for elegantly catered events: instead have everyone sit around a pizza. It's impossible to stand on one's dignity while eating pizza. You want everyone out of their authority roles, eating together like kids in a family.

This works surprisingly well at de-escalating tense situations. One guy was in charge of a community Little League, and at the start of the season all the coaches had to sit down together to figure out the rosters. People get fanatic about the Little League, all the coaches knew the best players and nobody wanted to give up the good ones. Yet the teams needed to be balanced somehow; in the past this meant wrangling sometimes until two o'clock in the morning.

This time the head of the league asked everyone over for pizza. All the coaches sat around and dug into the food, got good and messy, have a few laughes and then divvied up the players. They were out of there by 10:30. There were tense moments, but they never got around to the real fighting.

Monitoring

One day a student came in looking rattled. She'd been working with these ideas for a while; it wasn't easy for her, but she'd been working on it.

She'd been in a store, shopping for a present for her mother-in-law. Three clerks were behind the counter, talking and not paying the slightest attention to her. She asked if one could help her. A woman sized her up, sighed, rolled her eyes and tossed her a brochure.

My student responded like the Incredible Hulk: green skin, bulging muscles ripping out of her clothes. Feeling a little like she'd been taken over by aliens, she got herself out of the shop and wondered if she was losing her mind. OK, they were rude, but she was about to morph into a different species. They hadn't said anything. What was going on with her?

Actually, she wasn't losing her mind. She'd run into a phenomenon called "monitoring."

Monitoring gestures are subtle signals of contempt or disapproval, and they're far more powerful than you might think. They were first identified by a team of researchers, Albert and Alice Scheflen, who videotaped psychiatrists working with troubled families. They began noticing that some families had a way of pulling strings with their children that made the kids act crazier than they were to start with.

And it kept coming back to non-verbal monitors.
   Monitoring signals include:
   • The God-you're-stupid sigh
   • Rolling the eyes in exasperation or looking away
   • The disapproving sniff
   • A slight cough
   • The smirk
   • A mocking laugh
   • Brushing the nose

Think of the most shaming persons you ever knew: the eighth grade teacher with a glance like a whip, the tiny great-aunt whom everyone dreaded, the most feared maitre d' in New York. They're all so polite, but they somehow draw blood. It's done with monitoring signals.

These signals work like a psychic rabbit punch; they're fleeting and sometimes nearly subliminal. You may be negotiating your way through a trying situation, staying on track and keeping yourself in hand: then someone smirks at your good faith gesture. You want blood. You don't want to reason, you don't want to talk any more, you want to slap him silly.

You haven't lost your mind. You've just been monitored, and inarticulate fury is a typical response.

People doing monitoring are usually unaware that they're doing it. If you call them on it they probably won't know what you're talking about. In studies by Scheflen and Scheflen, researchers tried to explain the behavior to families and showed them videotapes of themselves monitoring. The families didn't get it. The Scheflens would replay the action over and over; some of the families never got it.

People who have been monitored aren't always angry; sometimes they feel mortified. They feel shamed, even when they're not quite sure just what it is they should be ashamed of. They may back away from the maitre d' in confusion, take the table by the kitchen door and then leave an oversized tip, just as if the business was all their own fault.

The Scheflens' found that monitoring is likely to make someone abruptly stop what they were doing, often without realizing it. It wouldn't matter if the action was right, wrong, or perfectly justified: when monitored, they'd drop it.

One office was having trouble with management, and the workers gathered over lunch to discuss what they could do. The staff firebrand insisted they should write a petition and take it to the top. A freshly minted lawyer was among them, and she leaned back and gave a long, silent, sarcastic laugh. The firebrand shut up and didn't say another word for the rest of the meeting.

Someone else took the firebrand's suggestion and went to upper management with the problem and promptly got the matter resolved. It turned out management had no idea their new initiative upset anyone. But even though the firebrand was proved right, he remained silent and hesitant around the new lawyer. He still acted like someone who'd been shamed.

Much of the power in monitoring comes from its subliminal nature. You don't know what's hit you. One approach is to bring it up to a conscious level where you can see it and deal with it. It may still rattle your thinking, but you won't feel blind-sided and it needn't control you.

Sometimes it helps just to observe. In a meeting where psychological warfare was rampant, I counted twenty-eight monitors in a one-hour span. It was fast and furious, and I kept the running tally. It kept me clear-headed when everyone else was livid.

Another approach is to call things out in the open. This can be especially important in meetings, where monitoring can undermine your position in front of others.

One woman was doing a presentation, when a colleague sniffed and rolled his eyes. She asked him what was on his mind. He said nothing—and sniffed. She asked if he had hayfever. He said of course not, and sniffed. By now the other people in the meeting were staring at him. The next time he sighed and sniffed she reached over and put a box of Kleenex in front of him and kept on talking without a pause.

Humor works, too. I once watched a friend, Cal, succumb to monitoring with Phillip, whom Cal owed a favor. (Phillip was adept at reminding people when they were in his debt.) Phillip was visiting, so Cal offered to take him to lunch.

Phillip had lived in Paris and Hong Kong, but Cal lived in Phoenix, Arizona. French, Continental or Asian food was out, since there was no way Phoenix could compete. So Cal suggested Mexican.

Phillip sighed and said, "Oh—all right (sniff!)" Cal looked stricken. He offered Thai or Laotian. Phillip sighed, but insisted on Mexican (sniff!).

Cal began to look panicked, but whatever he suggested, Phillip insisted on Mexican (with a sniff and a sigh). Trapped like a rat, Cal could only oblige. He dropped a hundred dollars on a gourmet Mexican lunch, knowing full well he would never live it down. Cal had not only failed to repay the debt, but he was deeper in hock than when he started.

A situation like this is basically absurd, so feel free to play with it. My suggestion to Cal next time was to insist he'd made a mistake; the Mexican restaurant had burned down. In fact, every Mexican restaurant had burned down. It was a very sad occasion: so how about West Coast cuisine?

Politicians monitor each other during debates, and sometimes even monitor themselves. "I assure you, no new taxes!" followed by a quick nose brush. The Scheflens discovered that sometimes when people lie or do something they're not proud of, they actually monitor themselves.

Now, is monitoring ever valid? Certainly. Listen to the audience when a play is really bad: you can hear slight coughs echoing up and down the house. The actors are dying up there but the fact remains, it's a bad play and the audience doesn't like it.

Similarly, if you try to weasel out of Aunt Harriet's luncheon, one of your relatives who knows what you're up to may suddenly start rubbing his nose. Take it with good grace—you've been busted. Be glad he doesn't say anything more.

Is there ever a time when it's all right for *you* to do monitoring? No. It makes no difference how annoyed you are, how bad they are or how richly it's deserved. Your nose may itch madly, begging to be rubbed. Supress the urge. Monitoring signals are loaded and you need to avoid them.

Here's the reason. If you make a mistake and monitor someone who has done nothing wrong, you can get a reaction you're not prepared for. If this is someone who is justified and who actually has been striving to get through to you, you may lose them completely. They may walk out of negotiations or out of your life, convinced there's no point in even trying.

Monitoring can create an irretrievable situation. I know how to do a great many things, but there's nothing in my bag of tricks that can bring that person back. Say what you think, but don't monitor.

Incidentally, if you were thinking of using monitoring deliberately to control people, forget it. The Scheflens found these signals truly were ingrained and couldn't be faked. They hired actors to stage monitoring; this had no effect. Either monitoring is genuine, done without thinking, or it seems to have no effect at all.

Progress

It's a gnarly business, trying to hold to problem-solving. Life and other people will not make it particularly easy for you.

The important thing is to keep trying, not to wait until you're perfect or freeze for fear of doing things wrong. Of course sometimes things will go wrong, but you have to be in motion to get back on track. A plane doesn't fly on course in one direction. It starts on course, veers off, corrects the trajectory, veers again, and keeps correcting itself until it lands. The plane that never leaves the runway can never correct its trajectory.

It's fine to make mistakes as long as you learn from them: try anything, as long as it isn't the same thing you've tried fruitlessly a dozen times before. That will put you in motion and give you the chance to move forward so you can watch for openings and correct your course. To wait until your behavior is perfect is to give yourself nothing to work with.

This system isn't about perfection; it's about the great human endeavor of trial and error.

Level one is actually not a very saintly place. It doesn't ask you to be kind, generous, compassionate or wise. These are all fine qualities, but problem-solving can exist without them. Wisdom may happen, I have nothing against it; however, wisdom isn't required for you to put your life in order. All that's needed for problem-solving is the ability to stop yourself from doing harm. That's all, but it's really quite a lot.

It requires a good deal of judgment to stop yourself from doing harm, keeping yourself from committing the small slights as well as the major offenses. It also requires integrity.

By this I mean integrity in the deeper sense of the word; a wholeness, being integrated, not divided against yourself. It means accepting the good and the bad in yourself, because those nagging little demons will trip you every time. Demons ("You're a bad mother!" "You'll never amount to much!") are central among the invisible factors that drive us to level two. They're primal forces like an ocean current—sometimes a rip tide, sometimes an undertow, always a danger to the swimmer.

Integrity is the antidote, but integrity comes demons and all. I have to admit that when thwarted or in pain I'm not, perhaps, at my rational best. If I'm looking for sainthood, I've just flunked; but if I'm looking for a functional life, this behavior is good enough.

Integrity allows you to admit your flaws, springing you from the trap of perfectionism and the automatic defensiveness that comes with it. Defensive people aren't stable; they're jumpy and quick to attack or defend. There's no point in saying this is bad; it's simply the cost of feeling defensive. Being imperfect and feeling not-defensive is a lot more productive and easier on the soul.

Generosity, compassion and kindness are emotions that only stable people can afford for more than a passing moment. With demons gnawing, generosity becomes perverted into patronization. Compassion becomes pity, reminding other people how small they are. No healthy person will thank us for it, and often it will get us a fight, or resentment, or a clever bit of sabotage when we're yanked, self-satisfied, off our pedestals.

Integrity keeps us grounded and level one is a grounded place. It's OK if you fall, it's not so far to earth and the pits of hell aren't waiting there. It's OK if you make a mistake, you can make up for it and do it right next time. You get a second chance, because as long as you're alive, there's always the opportunity to get it right.

Problem-solving isn't glorious, but it's a very decent place to be.

What to Remember

- **There is no staying at level one.** Life will shift us, and we need to be prepared to shift back. Practice is everything.

- **Before you can shift other people** you need to shift yourself. As Bevel said, we expect other people to be better than we are, and they're not. You can only lead from the front.

- **No problem can be solved as long as we defer responsibility.** Our problems in life are for us to solve, even if someone else ought to act better.

- **Common pressures** that will cause a shift for the worse include frustration, accusation, threatened boundaries and monitoring signals.

- **Sharing food**, especially hands-on, messy food, can cut tension and shift people towards comraderie.

- **Monitors are shaming signals** that include: the God-you're-stupid sigh, the annoyed sniff, rolling the eyes, a slight cough, smirking, or a quick brush of the nose. Shaming can provoke a volatile reaction both in yourself and others and should be carefully avoided.

- **Before a slide into unhealthy conflict**, you may find yourself in the transition zone: you're about to act out, but haven't yet. A miss is as good as a mile. If you can find your way back to problem-solving without having acted out, then count it as a victory.

- **Problem-solving isn't about being perfect:** it's about being able to correct your trajectory.

What Works Where

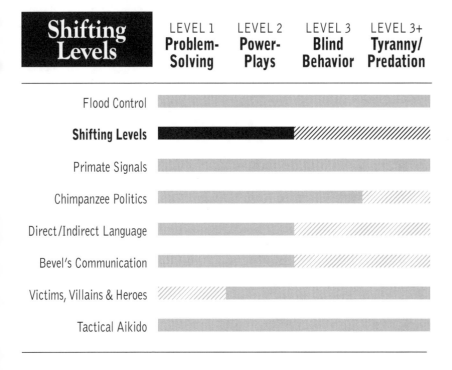

Shifting Levels	LEVEL 1 Problem-Solving	LEVEL 2 Power-Plays	LEVEL 3 Blind Behavior	LEVEL 3+ Tyranny/Predation
Flood Control				
Shifting Levels				
Primate Signals				
Chimpanzee Politics				
Direct/Indirect Language				
Bevel's Communication				
Victims, Villains & Heroes				
Tactical Aikido				

Shifting to Healthy Conflict happens readily at level two. By level three people become stuck in place, so shifting tactics will not work there; but they're quite effective at level two.

Chapter Four

The Ape and I

Small town Southerners, talking about the mayor: "But now, Sam, you know dat all he do is big-belly round and tell other folks what tuh do. He loves obedience out of everybody under de sound of his voice." "You kin feel a switch in his hand when he's talkin' to yuh..."

—Zora Neale Hurston, *Their Eyes Were Watching God*

Nanci Newton, a colleague of mine from Chimera self-defense, had studied primates in grad school and spent her days in the company of gorillas that out-weighed her by several hundred pounds. To survive this assignment she learned gorilla dominance signals. A 400-pound gorilla would rear and thunder her way, she'd face him down in gorilla-speak and he would go away quietly. At night she staffed the front desk at a battered women's shelter, and every now and then some thundering brute would storm inside to drag his woman home. To survive this assignment, my colleague would turn on the same gorilla signals, face down the brute and walk him out the door.

I was fascinated by what she could do with gorilla-speak. It was some time later that Nanci mentioned she was 4'11". I'm 5'9" and had never noticed she was shorter than I was.

Gorilla-speak is very good stuff. It impresses people who need to be impressed, calms people who need to be calmed and generally settles down bad situations. If a situation is veering into trouble, gorilla-speak can bring it back.

As an added bonus, primate signaling can get through to people who are flooding so badly they can't hear a word you say. Remember, flooding shuts down the higher parts of the brain, including the language centers. However, primate signals still work, even though so much of the higher brain has shut down.

Gorillas and chimps can't communicate with words because their jaws are designed for biting rather than talking. They primarily use a form of body language. This is different from the 'body talk' fad that swept the country. Primate signals will not say if a stranger at a party secretly craves your body. In gorilla terms, a simple nudge in the ribs will do.

The signals mentioned here are drawn largely from primatology; after all, we human are primates. We may be the Lexus edition of the great apes, but the patterns run close to form. Ape language we seem to have inherited wholesale. In fact, primate signals are so powerful, if there is ever a difference between what you say in English and what you say in gorilla, the English will be discarded and the gorilla-speak will be believed.

These signals are so crucial that a gaff in ape communication can ruin anything you try to accomplish. An inadvertent show of nervousness will undermine your credibility, while a slip of belligerence will ruin rapport. You may not even know what you've done, only that the situation has suddenly gone downhill.

It's crucial that you have ape signals firmly under control and know what these signals communicate. In a later chapter I insist that honesty is a wise policy, that lying undermines your own tactics. However, in the case of ape signaling, lying works. Lying with authority posture is the only way you can stand before an angry crowd and convince them they need to worry about *you*. You can shake in your tracks and project a solid presence, or be livid without anyone being the wiser for it. At times, when it's needed, apes lie through their teeth. They project confidence when terrified and calm when they're furious. Ape lying works. You do it, too.

In conflict, there are three main types of primate signals: belligerence signals, submissive signals and what I'll call authority signals. Belligerence and submissive gestures are generally sure to make things worse. Authority signals make things better. These are easy techniques, so you'll want to have them down.

Primate Belligerence

This is the Red Queen from *Through the Looking Glass*, doing belligerent display. There's the jutting jaw, a ridge of muscle over the eyes, while the mouth is open, showing teeth (grinding teeth or chomping a cigar will do as well). The Red Queen is also pointing her finger. Shaking your finger in someone's face happens to be one of the single fastest ways to start a fistfight in the continental United States.

The jutting jaw and forehead ridge result in the 'bulldog' look, which is classic belligerence. You'll notice the Red Queen looks a lot like a bulldog. Some people spend so much time with the 'bulldog' look their face grows into it. J. Edgar Hoover, Winston Churchill, Jimmy Cagney and Nikita Khrushchev all had that 'bulldog' look, and they came to look like brothers as they got older.

Another belligerent signal is the belly display, which the Red Queen also shows. The blue collar version is the beer-belly swagger, like a redneck cop in a bad movie. This is strictly human; gorillas don't have beer-bellies, but you'll find it puts your hackles up just the same.

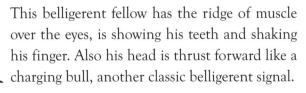

This belligerent fellow has the ridge of muscle over the eyes, is showing his teeth and shaking his finger. Also his head is thrust forward like a charging bull, another classic belligerent signal.

Another belligerence sign is a sharp, snarling voice. There's a Southern saying: 'That's the bark with the bite in it.' Even dogs make this distinction. A happy, cheerful dog has a high, light yap, but a dog about to bite has a low, guttural snarl.

Anything becomes a threat in that snarling tone of voice, even someone's name. You've been at a store and heard a mother snarl, 'Jimmy! Get over here!' It's the voice moms get when they've really lost it.

If this person is you, stop in mid-sentence and bring your voice back to normal. The snarling voice is going much too far.

Another part of belligerent display is slamming things. Chimpanzees rip off tree branches and bash them on the ground. Khrushchev pounded his shoe at the U.N. General Assembly. Judges pound gavels. Angry customers slam the counter, adolescents slam doors, and you, at some point, have probably slammed out of the house. It's a statement.

It's important to remember that belligerence signals are all about display. It's supposed to be intimidating. If you're on the receiving end your blood pressure will probably jump as if you're actually under threat, but remember, display is different from actual harm. Winston Churchill might chomp his cigar, set his jaw and growl, but he never bit anyone in the throat. He might have tapped into a visceral fear, but it wasn't real. It was just for show.

Now, belligerence typically begets belligerence. So if you're in a bad situation, belligerence signals will make things worse.

I have a friend of high rank in the martial arts, who is bi-polar (sometimes called manic-depressive). Two of us managed to get her to the hospital in her manic phase, but there were some tense moments waiting in the emergency room. She was in a great mood (witty, in fact), but loud and chaotic. Guards who didn't know better would order her to settle down. Well, manic people don't settle down, so the guards felt defied and the situation escalated.

Once two burly guards bellied in, shoulder to shoulder, and squared off in front of her. Her eyes lit up. She wasn't intimidated; she saw this as a black belt test, and two large attackers were a great honor. One of us grabbed her, and the other shoved these guys out of the room before she bowed and tore loose. She was really disappointed. She looked like a pup who'd had her chew toy taken away. She'd perk up whenever someone came to the door, and looked disappointed when it was just an intern.

This kind of behavior is so loaded that one hospital started using females guards in the emergency room because they were so were much better at de-escalation. Before, a male guard would storm in, barking orders with his hand on his gun. Naturally, he'd get a fight. A female guard was more likely to walk in with her hands open, talking to people. She would get people to calm down and take a seat.

Knowing belligerence signals also can help you stop a problem before it starts. A mechanical engineer was on site with the crew from hell, a family outfit that fought like the Hatfields and McCoys. The engineer would scan the project, watch for belligerence signs and separate people at the first sign of trouble. He got a reputation for being psychic. They were amazed that on a four-acre site he could appear just in time to head off a confrontation. After a while they wanted to know how he did it.

On rare occasions, belligerence signals can get someone's attention when nothing else works. Once, after a car wreck, a small woman had to get a big, burly guy to stop wandering dazed, into the intersection. He was too big to wrestle down, so she squared off and barked, 'George, sit down—Now!' George sat down. He'd start to stand up, she'd bark again, and he'd sit back down. That's how she held him until the ambulance came.

Primate Submissiveness

The flip side of belligerence is submissive signaling.

The nervous fellow on the left is exhibiting submissive posture. He's twisting his fingers in a knock-kneed pose, with his body turned away from the man addressing him. This twisted posture is known as five-point indirectness. The five points on the body are the face, the point of each shoulder and the point of each hip. In contrast, notice how the other man is facing him directly. The twisted posture signals fear or submission; the animated expression is another submissive signal.

Wringing the hands—which is of course, submissive—is a version of self-clutching. People may grab onto one wrist, hug their arms around themselves, or get a white-knuckle grip on a steno pad. Small, frightened chimpanzees do similar things. It doesn't look good in humans.

Humans doing submissive posturing get treated very badly. Submissive posture in the great apes will generally calm a fight. It says, 'You're big and powerful; I'm small and helpless. Don't hurt me.' Generally speaking, apes will leave the weaker one alone. Humans, unfortunately, get more aggressive. With humans the fight gets worse.

A human doing submissive posture is variously seen as stupid, sneaky, lying or inept. It is viewed as a flag for dishonesty or incompetence; therefore such people deserve to be hurt. Uriah Heep would bob and wring his hands. He wasn't considered helpful, he was considered odious.

In this picture Uriah Heep has his body hunched small, sitting on the edge of his chair and playing with his fingers. He's also doing head-cocking. Think of the RCA Victor dog "Listening to his master's voice." Now, there is a different kind of head tilt that's an intense kind of peering, like the Marlborough Man sizing up a horse. It's easy to tell the difference; one looks keen and intelligent, while the other looks simpering.

Anyone under pressure can slip into nervous submissive signals, which unfortunately is when we can least afford it. Feeling frightened at times is normal; just don't show it with submissive signals.

The foolish grin, with no reason to smile, is also submissive posturing; Uriah is doing that as well. In chimps it's called a 'fear grin.' This is the sickly smile people sometimes get when they're under attack. These people aren't happy, they're frightened.

There's a photo taken of Neville Chamberlain—known to history as 'The Great Appeaser'—at his meeting with Hitler in Munich. Chamberlain is shown nervously rubbing his wrist. These were arguably the most disastrous negotiations in modern history. Chamberlain had a bigger army, navy, and air force than Hitler, but Hitler decided he could push his luck. It was not the time for submissive signs.

The caption for the photo on the left is "The New Woman—Wash Day" with the young wife lording it over her hapless mate. The year was 1901 and the photographer clearly didn't look forward to women getting the vote. Again the husband's body is crouched small, while the wife is open and expansive. She faces him while he's twisted away. He's wringing the wash rather than wringing his hands, and he's also doing head-cocking. It's clear who wears the knickers in the family.

There were photos of a controversial researcher who was sometimes hailed as a hero and sometimes pilloried as a fraud and a cheat. In a critical story the scientist was shown clutching a microphone, gazing up over his shoulder at the questioner and smiling weakly. He looked like a lying little rat.

Later a different story portrayed him as a hero; the picture showed him expansive, calm, square shouldered and relaxed. I checked his tie and the position of the microphones: both shots were taken at the same news conference. Those two photos conveyed vastly different impressions, one of which was disastrous.

Many female flirtatious gestures are actually submissive signals, and they don't come across as very bright. Toying with hair is a version of self-grooming; it's the human equivalent of picking lice. In a similar way, men fiddle with their watch bands or nervously jingle change in their pockets. Fidgeting, jangly jewelry or fluttering gestures are also submissive signals.

Smiling when there's no reason to smile, giggling at inappropriate times or using a high, breathy voice are all submissive signals. These gestures make it virtually impossible to be taken seriously. You may have the IQ of Einstein, but you'll be written off as a dip.

White, middle-class American women do an inordinate amount of submissive posturing, even when they don't mean it. In the office this can cause a lot of problems. One woman, a technical expert, continually did submissive signals: playing with jewelry, toying with her hair, self-clutching, the whole nine yards. She was also brilliant and nearly irreplaceable.

She was overdue for a raise and went in to talk to her boss about it. She sat down, fidgeted, played with her hair and said in a high, breathy voice, "If I don't get my raise, I'm leaving." Her boss, a big blustery man, laughed it off (monitoring). Two weeks later she turned in her resignation. Her boss was thunderstruck. He had no idea she was serious and he couldn't afford to lose her. For her part, she couldn't understand why he hadn't believed her.

Inadvertent submissive signals will undermine you as a manager or even as a parent. You can't effectively give an order; you won't be taken seriously. A command with submissive signals is typically considered a request, an option, nothing very important. A teenager will ignore it and an underling will put it at the bottom of his list. This will infuriate the manager or mom who will think she's being disrespected. The anger will confound the subordinate, who had no warning that this order was meant to be taken seriously.

Leadership Signals

So if belligerent or submissive posture will both make things worse, what will make things better? The great apes have a solution, which for lack of a better word can be referred to as leadership posture.

This is Lincoln in full authority pose. Leadership posture has a relatively impassive face. It can be friendly enough, but it's not animated like the submissive pose. The stance is upright and open, with basic good posture, taking up one body's width of space. There's five-point directness, with all five points front and center. Nothing is twisted or turned away.

The standard American business suit will hold leadership posture whether or not anyone's inside it. A business suit isn't made to bend. It will hang wrong if the owner slips out of leadership stance.

In authority posture, the face shows little emotion but the eyes are alert and intelligent. I once spoke with a business owner who said outrageous things in a newspaper interview and still had the reporter in the palm of her hand. The accompanying photo was terrific. I asked her how she managed it. She said, "Smile with your eyes. Don't smile with your mouth—you'll look like a used car salesman. Smile with your eyes." This is particularly helpful in situations where your authority is in question.

The leadership voice is low and resonant, coming from the diaphragm. You may have a naturally high, breathy voice. Everyone has a high register and a low register; use your low register. If you feel your voice getting higher under stress, take a deep breath and bring your voice down again.

The voice of authority, taken too far, turns into The Authority Drone. This is why it can be so hard sometimes to stay awake in lectures or to listen to Senate hearings on the radio. There's no need to take things that far. Keep your voice low, but stay lively enough that people can bear to listen to you.

In leadership posture, the movements are smooth and deliberate. The feet are planted, the body is upright but the posture is rather relaxed, not rigid. If there is tension, it doesn't show. Think of Cary Grant walking into a room.

Authority posture doesn't go with the person who is afraid of losing power or trying to seize power. It goes with the person who *has* power.

With authority signals, people assume you know what you're doing. Leaders or experts live in authority posture. Doing this, you'll be read as intelligent, capable, responsible and honest. This posture will not automatically make you all these things, but people will assume you're quite sound. In fact, there have been any number of people with splendid poise and resonant baritones who have taken command without a brain in their heads. No reason you can't do it, too.

Of all the techniques, authority posture is the fastest, easiest way to get someone else back to sensible behavior. These signals need to be part of your wardrobe.

An intern had been assisting a volatile surgeon and had made a mistake during the operation. No harm was done but the intern knew there would be blood the moment she walked out of the changing room. Through the frosted glass she could see the surgeon pacing up and down in a fury. She gathered herself, walked out in full authority posture, put out her hand and said, "I'm *so* sorry," in a resonant voice. The surgeon mumbled something and told her to forget it. That was all.

The engineer who intercepted fights in the wildcat crew always stayed in authority posture. It didn't matter if he was angry or nervous or ready to tear his hair. It didn't matter how he felt, it mattered what signals he gave.

When you do authority posture, it's crucial that you don't let a single belligerent or submissive signal leak through. A single anxious signal can undermine everything. Check your own body language when you're angry or nervous. You may have an unconscious habit that would give you away, like clenching your fists or fidgeting without knowing it.

Your hands are most likely to give you away. If your hands tend to fidget or clutch things when you're nervous, imagine welding the sides of your hands to the table; now leave your hands melted to the table. Don't move them. If you pick something up, put it back down and melt your hands again. If your hands aren't moving they can't get you into trouble.

Authority posture one notch up is the pose of the hero or titan. There's still five-point directness and a relatively impassive face, but now the body takes up more space. The feet are planted with arms akimbo. This conveys yet greater authority, still without crossing into belligerence.

This is Henry VIII in full authority posture. It's also a favorite superhero pose, a model of benign power: truth, justice and the American way. Many African-American women are great at this; they can grow half a foot before your eyes. Observe anyone you think of as a calm, confident, "natural born" leader. You'll find he or she spends much of the day in one version or another of a calm, steady authority posture.

In a bad situation, it can be useful to slowly ratchet up the authority signals. I once faced an angry man who had side-swiped my car and was trying to intimidate me into dropping the case. He was in full belligerent display: charging head, thundering voice, shaking his finger in my face. I didn't say a word—in fact I was flooding and didn't know what to say. I also couldn't get a word in, so I went into authority posture. While he shouted, I looked at him levelly and squared to face him with five point directness. I took all the expression off my face and relaxed my hands out of a nervous grip.

He kept yelling. I continued to watch him calmly and put one hand on my hip. Then I slowly put the other hand on my other hip. His voice began to drop to a normal tone. I held my pose. To my surprise, he began to fidget and glance away still while insisting he was right. Then he ducked his head and did a little shuffle with his feet: he was doing submissive posture to me! Finally he made an excuse and hurried away. Our lawyers worked out the rest.

The stoneface is authority posture taken to the limit. The body is motionless and the face has no expression at all. The eyes hardly blink. It is intimidating and rather nerve-wracking, but not provocative.

Sometimes stoneface is used as a negotiating trick to unsettle the opposition and drive the price down. Don't fall for it. Mentally catalog the symptoms and keep your flooding under control. The stoneface is just another display, like belligerence; don't let yourself be unnerved by it.

Let's say you must present your case to the chairman of the board, J. Stoneface. Stoneface is known for his low glower and his tendency to kill ficus trees by sheer proximity. You naturally feel nervous, but you've prepared a sound presentation.

You walk in to Stoneface's office and present your idea with style, intelligence and articulation. Stoneface stares at you, not moving a muscle. You come to the end of your presentation. Stoneface continues to look at you. He grunts.

You sense your idea has not gone over well. You re-explain it, covering all the major points. You smile winningly and start to fidget. There's still no response and you can feel yourself losing ground even as you speak. Your smile becomes ridiculous and your voice inches higher, and you're starting to babble like a fool. Stoneface finally mutters something and you leave, deflated.

This is not a case of temporary imbecility, but a dominance/submission pattern. The stoneface triggered a submissive, appeasing response. As you talk you can hear yourself lose credibility. The power difference deepens into a chasm. Even if Stoneface accepts your idea (he may have liked it all along), you'll get much less than you originally expected. Submissive signals destroy your bargaining power.

You can't change Stoneface's behavior. There is no signal that will cause his face to break into a sunburst of golden smiles. Besides, it's a cheap trick and he probably knows what he's doing. Instead, concentrate on the presentation, with or without his feedback. Ask questions. Have a follow-up prepared so that you can go on to the next point if you don't get a response. When you're ready to stop, stop. Relax in authority posture.

It also helps to mentally translate ape signals into English. He pulls a stoneface. You note, "OK, he says he's Mr. Big." This is not a shock. Fifteen minutes later he's still insisting that he is Mr. Big. The point is duly noted. But by staying in authority posture, you show you can handle the pressure.

What You See Is Not What You Get

Being able to read primate signals will give you the chance to clear away some of the smoke and mirrors that people use in psychological warfare. You may not like what you see, but at least you can see clearly.

I once watched an old-style Chicago cop give a talk on self-defense. The people waiting in the audience demonstrated the usual random mix of signals: some comfortable in authority posture, some neutral, some twisted in nervous submissive.

The policeman took the floor. He was six foot four, big bellied, and planted his feet with five-point directness. He started talking in a low, booming voice, telling gruesome stories that always ended with the victim dead.

As he took the floor most people in the audience cocked their heads in attention/submission. As he described (in great detail) the hapless fate of these victims, the audience began to show more submissive posturing: curling up smaller in their chairs, ducking their heads, clutching their bodies, playing with hair and jewelry. Although all the hapless victims were female, even the men in the audience began showing submissive signals.

As the audience grew more submissive, the policeman grew more belligerent—pounding his fist into his hand, jutting out his jaw and throwing his belly around. Yet in all these cases the cops were useless; no one was protected and the citizens were just dead meat.

When it came time for questions, a few members of the audience tentatively put up their hands and smiled submissively, and continued to grin while he told them about the grisly fate that awaited them.

That cop sold a lot of Mace that night. People lined up to buy it in full submissive posture and smiled when they gave him the money.

This was psychological warfare, the cop against the citizens. People paid money for this.

Primate signals often mask a variety of contradictory moves. Often in conflict, what you see is not what you get.

On the south side of Chicago, the men would square off to fight while women might step in as peacemakers. However, black and white women tended to handle the job in completely different ways.

The men would usually fight using roughly the same procedure. They would face off in belligerent stance, with threatening voices, jutting jaws, lots of blood and thunder. They'd do full belligerent display but stay just out of reach. After all, fighting on the south side was a dangerous thing, since you never quite knew who you were dealing with. So there would be a good deal of display—so as not to lose face—while staying out of reach so as not to lose blood. Meanwhile, each combatant was likely to have a proverbial antenna up, looking for an honorable way out of the fight.

Often women would appear to break it up and extricate their men from the fight, but black women were often more effective. Black women tended to arrive in authority posture while reaching their hands out in a soothing way. They'd be able to negotiate an end to the fight. The men could then retreat with honor, since they only stopped because of their women.

In contrast, white women all too often would arrive doing submissive signals, begging their men to drop the fight. In that case, the man might turn around *and hit the girlfriend*, berating her for butting in. That became his exit from the fight. He'd leave his erstwhile enemy standing there while he cursed and threatened the smaller woman he knew wouldn't hurt him. It was a very cheap move. Because it was done in belligerence posture, these guys walked away looking manly. It was a particularly shabby exit.

The crucial difference in these cases was the ape signaling, not race per se. I can't recall ever having seen a black woman step into a situation like that doing submissive signals. Meanwhile, if a woman of either race arrived in full belligerence it seemed to propel the men into an active fistfight, especially if she swung first.

What to Remember

Primate signaling is one of the make-or-break techniques. If you master these skills you can abruptly become better at handling conflicts. If you continue to make primate mistakes you will get unnecessary problems. These are easy skills. You want them working in your favor.

- **Either belligerence or submissive** posture will cause a situation to deteriorate. Authority posture will improve it.

- **Avoid belligerence signals:** Barking voice, furrowed ridge over the eyes, jutting jaw, the head thrust forward in the 'charging bull' posture, showing teeth, pounding things, the 'bulldog' look.

- **Avoid submissive signals:** Crouching, self-clutching, fidgeting, five-point indirectness, high/breathy voice, giggling, grinning or a foolishly animated face.

- **Use authority signals:** Upright posture, five-point directness, impassive expression, alert eyes. Plant your feet, smile with your eyes. If the conflict is still intense, move point by point to a higher level of authority posture: hands on hips, expressionless face. Stop moving. Say less, rather than more.

- **Have all primate signals under control.** A single belligerent or submissive 'leak' can undermine your presentation as badly as if you were quaking on your feet. People will zero in on the one faulty gesture, which will undercut anything else you try to do.

- **Signals don't have to be real** to be effective. They're just signals, no more, no less. This is not a window on the soul. You don't have to *be* calm and confident, you only have to look like it.

- **Don't be impressed** by belligerence signals. Observe them but stay detached. Buying in will only make matters worse.

- **Watch for submissive signals** in someone who is intimidated or who is losing a power struggle. This is a way of gauging a conflict.

- **Observe leadership signals** in anyone presenting power or statesmanship, but don't let that cloud your judgment. Remember, authority signals don't necessarily prove someone to be intelligent or capable; he or she may only look the part.

What Works Where

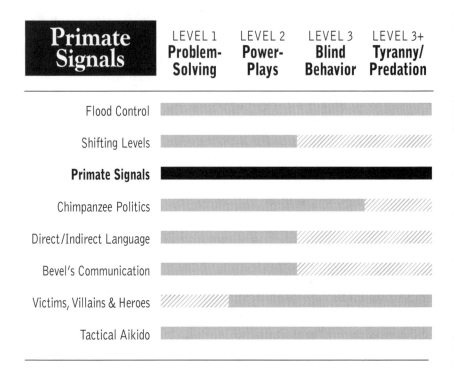

Primate Signals	LEVEL 1 Problem- Solving	LEVEL 2 Power- Plays	LEVEL 3 Blind Behavior	LEVEL 3+ Tyranny/ Predation
Flood Control	███	███	███	███
Shifting Levels	███	░░░	░░░	░░░
Primate Signals	███	███	███	███
Chimpanzee Politics	███	███	███	░░░
Direct/Indirect Language	███	░░░	░░░	░░░
Bevel's Communication	███	░░░	░░░	░░░
Victims, Villains & Heroes	░░░	███	███	███
Tactical Aikido	███	███	███	███

Primate Signals are helpful in nearly any kind of conflict.

Chapter Five

Chimpanzee Politics

As long as we're on the topic of chimps, we may as well talk about business.

Chimpanzee politics are important in business as well as in schools, families or other organizations. Like us, chimpanzees are smart, individual and live in herds. We humans were never equipped to survive alone. We have no fangs or claws, no great ability to run, swim or climb. A lone human, outside a group, is essentially leopard bait. Our survival depends on our ability to work together, but our individuality can make that difficult.

Chimpanzees work out this problem through hierarchies, the chimp equivalent of the organizational pyramid. However, chimps have two different systems in play, which both have echoes in human affairs. Some of the most insightful work in this field was done by the renowned primatologist Frans DeWaal. More revelations came from the brave female researchers who worked their way into wild chimpanzee groups to gain first-hand accounts of just what was going on.

Chimpanzee politics are fascinating and complex, as are human politics. Since a chapter can hardly do justice to the field, this will only touch on the crucial points that can make or break a conflict situation.

Who's Where on the Food Chain

The first system is the classic pecking order, which is primarily for chimpanzee males. There's an Alpha chimp, then a Beta, Gamma and so on. The hierarchy is held in place from the top down: the Alpha gets to rough up the Beta, the Beta gets to lean on the Gamma, and on down the ladder. That's how you know who's boss, because he gets to hurt you.

Alpha

Beta

Gamma

Delta

Most of us have worked at places like this. It's the classic 'male management style' that not every male believes in and not every female has renounced. It's management as practiced by the marines, hard-core MBA schools and various households around the country.

Rank and power are central to the structure. A new manager takes over a marketing department and publicly pounds out several of his most productive workers. In fact, he keeps this up for months even as they're trying to please him. The reason is that the most productive guys are potential rivals of the Alpha and he wants to make sure they know who's boss. The pounding is done publicly, so that the rest of the department can get the point as well. He will only stop once he's sure they know their 'place.'

This isn't just done out of willful malice; there's a problem inherent in the ladder system. The structure allows for only one chimp per rung, so if a chimp wishes to move up (and who wouldn't) he has to displace the chimp above him. This means the upper chimps have to keep an eye on the lower chimps and be ready to fend off advances—hence the pounding. In a sense the whole system is inherently unstable, with the lower chimps inevitably threatening to oust the higher chimps, and the upper chimps hammering down to keep them in their place.

If, however, you're the one getting pounded, you no doubt want this to stop. It's a chimpanzee problem, so primate signaling works quite well. Stay in authority posture at all times: upright posture, relatively impassive face, low, resonant voice. Submissive signals will make this worse and even a wisp of belligerence will complicate matters. Authority signals communicate that you are honorable, stable, and that fighting isn't necessary. You don't have to be boss to have authority; you can be a worthy, sound subordinate.

As odd as it may sound, this primate needs to be assured that you know he or she is the boss. So say so. Accept directions with words like, "Got it. You're the boss." Use phrases like "Yes sir," and "No sir." That may sound old-fashioned, but this is an old-fashioned system. The higher chimps need to know that you accept their place on the hierarchy. You don't have to like it—liking it has little to do with the pecking order. But you need to acknowledge that they have more clout than you do, which is true.

At some point you may be in a position to change the system; certainly one can hope that you won't pass it on yourself. But if you are in the process of getting pounded, your priority is to get the pounding to stop, not to reform millennia of hierarchy. Get the pounding to stop first. Reform world order later.

Hazing

Every group needs new blood, even a ladder structure. When a new chimp is ready to join the hierarchy, the older ones will unite to make the young one's life miserable. It's not unlike a hazing process, and if the new one makes it through he wins a rung on the ladder and gets to start moving up in earnest.

Clearly we can see similar things in human society. To join an old-style male institution one often goes through hazing and the more elite the society, the worse the hazing. That's what boot camp is all about. Boot camp is bad for the army, worse for Marines and nearly unbearable for Green Berets or Navy SEALs. The same is true for elite schools or businesses. When I did a talk at the University of Virginia, the grad students informed me that their MBA students had a 100% divorce rate. That meant if you went in married, you would be divorced by the time you got out. That was considered the mark of a top school.

Other elite hierarchies do the same thing. You may have wondered why a medical intern should be kept up 36 hours at a stretch and how this might make him or her a better healer. Of course it doesn't, it's just ladder protocol. Chiropractic schools who wish to be taken as seriously as M.D.s, will brutalize their students nearly as badly to show they're just as good.

Checking the Competition

On the ladder, male chimps constantly check who is where and who is moving up on them. Will James was a working cowboy who wrote about life on the range early in the twentieth century. Cowboys lived in a group, did the same work, ate the same food and slept outside on the same cold ground, yet automatically created a hierarchy:

> "There was pride in the work and how each cowboy done it, and where there's pride there's always a little jealousy. That way each man was contesting against the other, each tried to be a better rider, roper, or cowman, and none was of the same standing.
>
> "The working hours was never thought of, on account that with them a man could show what he was made of. The kind of horses he rode and how neat he throwed a rope all went for or against him to tell what kind of hand he was, and it kept him on the jump, because no matter how good he might of been there is always room for improvement in that game, and there could always be somebody that was a little better."

In some ways the hierarchy drove them to excellence and certainly kept them hard at work. There's no question there are things going for this system, but it's not the only way to live.

Cluster Hierarchy

Female chimps organize life entirely differently, with what's known as a cluster hierarchy. There may be only one Alpha, but the rest are arranged in groups of equals. It might look like this:

Alpha

Beta   Beta   Beta

Gamma   Gamma   Gamma

Delta   Delta   Delta

The different levels are true equals; one Beta is not more Beta than another. The hierarchy has more flexibility and less threat. If a Gamma moves up there are merely four Betas instead of three. Nobody need get displaced.

Now, another way to describe a cluster hierarchy is not to sketch it as a pyramid at all, but as a series of concentric circles. The Alpha isn't above but at the center of the group, and standing can be seen not by how high someone is, but by how central.

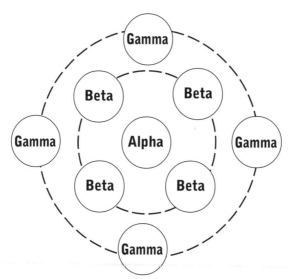

In *The Female Advantage,* Sally Helgesen wrote about women's management styles. In that book Frances Hesselbein, one of the most well-respected managers in the nation, mapped out her management system as interconnected concentric circles. It was disconcertingly similar to what primatologists were sketching in the wilds of Kenya.

While the ladder hierarchy gets enforced from the top down, the cluster hierarchy is essentially enforced from the bottom up: Betas respect and defer to the Alpha, the Alpha doesn't wring subservience from the Betas. Female chimps win respect not through intimidation but though social skills, ability and what we might call chimpanzee merit.

In clusters it makes less sense for higher chimps to lean on lower chimps, since intimidation wins fear rather than respect. In a cluster fear isn't a useful currency; respect is.

Deference and Care-taking

This smoothing deference can result in female rituals that make no sense to ladder males. Alice Walker, the Pulitzer Prize winning novelist, once interviewed Coretta Scott King. At the time Walker was a comparative unknown and something went wrong with Walker's tape recorder:

".... I lean forward to fix it, explaining with some vexation that I am the world's worst manipulator of simple gadgetry. Coretta charitably admits she's no genius with mechanical things either."

Here were two of the most dynamic women in the country insisting that they can't manage household electronics. In ladder terms, that's stupid. But this wasn't to be taken literally; in a cluster system deference is inclusive, not servile. By handling things this way neither party lost face.

In contrast, cartoonists do regular riffs on two guys peering at an engine, posturing over who knows more about carburetors when neither knows anything at all. In cluster terms, that's foolish, but it does make sense in a ladder system.

In a pecking order, to defer or admit you don't know something is to put yourself below the other person. On a food chain, that's suicide; you may as well hang a sign on yourself that says "Lunch." Therefore with ladders, the tendency is to assume knowledge you do not know or act with authority you may not have.

A similar problem occurs around care-taking. Cluster hierarchies do a lot of social care-taking: remembering birthdays, personal chit-chat, soft human things that seem to have no place in business. In a ladder hierarchy only inferiors do care-taking; underlings remember the boss's birthday, he doesn't remember theirs.

Misunderstandings

When these hierarchies cross it can get very messy. Lea was a project leader with an aero-space firm, with five male engineers and several consultants working under her. In feminine fashion, she would defer to them; if her subordinates were wrong, she would never contradict them. She would agree, bolster their egos and then lead them off in a more appropriate direction. Lea would have personal talks with all of them, air different problems and help make them feel at home. She would even tell them personal, vulnerable details of her life.

Courteous, kind leadership, no? It wrecked havoc with team unity. Because she deferred to the others they assumed they were more knowledgeable and important than she was. They stopped taking orders from her. They even proceeded to give her orders, then squabbled with each other over which of them was in charge. Since Lea wasn't the head of the hierarchy, someone else had to be.

Lea meant well, but she was doing exactly the wrong things for holding a ladder hierarchy in place.

Hazards

These two systems represent fully functioning world views, but they often fail to understand each other.

Women get exasperated and say, "What's wrong with this place? I'm good at what I do—Why can't I get a little respect around here?" These are the assumptions of the cluster chimp and have little meaning in a ladder world. In a pecking order, contradicting and competing would more likely to win respect.

Men are apt to find the same assumptions hopelessly naive. They often get exasperated with women who won't learn to 'play the game.' They tend to think that women only do this to be contrary, not that they're expecting a different, equally valid set of rules.

Now, it's important to make a distinction here. Most men understand the ladder, even if they refuse to play by those rules. Most women understand the cluster system, even if they choose the rough climb to the top. But at least both have an understanding of what it is they're rejecting.

The worst mistakes happen not when someone rejects a system, but when they don't even know it's there. For instance, people used to the pecking order may not register a cluster system at all. Not only don't they value it, they don't even notice it. There is no clear 'top' and they see no visible order. To them the department seems to run itself. Consequently, cluster leaders often are not taken seriously and may not be seen as real players. And since they're not players, they often get run over. Someone from the outside may dismiss the cluster Alpha, never noticing that he or she is essential. They have no idea they've removed the linchpin. The damage isn't noticed until the department stops functioning.

For example, Diance Nash was one of the great tacticians of the civil rights movement and a true cluster Alpha. She was nearly written out of history, partly because of sexism of course, but partly because she consistently deflected attention from herself and gave full credit to the group around her. She didn't particularly trouble with leadership positions, though she was the one people turned to in times of crisis. She preferred to be at the center of things rather than at the top looking down.

Nash had the rare ability to turn defeat into victory, a skill badly needed throughout the civil rights era. In time it became impossible for her to stay in the movement and she left after Selma, a victory she helped achieve. Once she left, the civil rights movement lost those needed skills. No one else seemed able to do what she could do.

So far as I can tell, the central leadership didn't particularly notice when Nash had to leave. They didn't seem to realize she was pivotal, or that it wasn't just co-incidence that her campaigns succeeded. Since she didn't command center stage, they didn't really see her.

A different kind of damage can occur if these two systems overlap. For instance, the aggressiveness of a ladder type can prove fatal to a cluster hierarchy. If you take one or two intense ladder types and drop them into a thriving, productive cluster, they can cut through that system like a knife through butter. The cluster hardly knows what hit them. Clusters can be so engaged in being inclusive, open and caring they fail to notice they're being mulched.

Ladder groups, on the other hand, can readily deal with aggressive newcomers; they get them all the time. They fight for a while, the newcomer gets beaten silly, then learns limits and settles down.

Clusters need to set limits, too. Limits are healthy, not just the province of the ladder types. Clusters need firm ways of setting standards and making unwelcome aggression stop. Someone—preferably someone with seniority—needs to take the newcomers aside and say, "You know when you told your teammates to shut up? We don't have that kind of thing here. Stop it. Now." Limits don't have to be brutal but they do have to be firm.

Knowledge and Power

Now, these two systems each have their gifts. For instance, the ladder hierarchy is the usual way to run an old-technology system like a factory or an army. The cluster hierarchy, however, tends to be better at high technology. This has to do with the way they use knowledge.

Both these groups can agree on one thing: knowledge is power. Since a cluster will get stronger if all peers are stronger, the obvious thing is to share knowledge and bring everyone up to speed. However, the opposite is true in a ladder hierarchy. In that case, knowledge is power, therefore you hoard it. You do not let the other people know what you know, because then they can do away with you.

This becomes a problem in the so-called 'Super Cop' syndrome. On a police force there might be one unusually effective cop, whom the administration would promote to management so he could create a new generation of Super Cops. But that didn't work, because if the Super Cop gave away his secrets of success then anyone else could be like him. So once put in charge, he would take command and *not* tell the others his secrets in order to protect his position.

Another problem with the ladder is that since knowledge was power, only the elite were allowed to have any. This is why some managers behave as if no one but themselves could have good ideas. Knowledge was honor and the prerogative of the elite; therefore lower types would be ignored.

Not listening can get quite dangerous at times. For instance, an airplane is run on a ladder hierarchy: the pilot is Alpha, the co-pilot is Beta, the head flight attendant is well down the ladder and the other flight attendants hardly count. There was a tape recording from a black box of a plane that crashed shortly after take-off. On it, the head flight attendant repeatedly tried to tell the pilot there was ice on the wings, while the pilot repeatedly disregarded her. He wouldn't even go and check for himself. That knowledge hierarchy proved very costly.

High Danger

In a cluster anyone is allowed to have knowledge and anyone can get that knowledge heard, which makes it the better choice in dangerous situations. For instance, an aircraft carrier—overwhelmingly male—incorporates elements of a cluster hierarchy. An aircraft carrier has to bring a plane down at high speeds on a small slab of metal in the middle of the ocean; if something goes wrong they lose the plane and probably the pilot. So if anyone on board spots trouble they have to be heard quickly, without going up through ranks.

The crew uses a more egalitarian style. For instance, even a small bit of metal can cause an accident, so the entire crew turns out for a safety check. Everyone, from the officers to the deck hands, walk shoulder to shoulder down the length of the ship.

Carriers also do the care-taking that's considered frivolous in a pecking order. One year, during budget cuts, the ships were to lose their on-board bakeries. Navy brass successfully argued that they needed to make their own birthday cakes in order to maintain morale; it would not do to have them flown in from outside. This is not what you'd see on the line at GM.

High Technology

Cluster values can pay off in the high tech world, especially when it comes to sharing knowledge. This became crucial at Apple, which was known for its innovation, technical excellence and egalitarian system.

Apple was led by Steve Jobs, who was largely a cluster Alpha. Perks and offices were egalitarian, the culture was open and anyone, including the newest hire, could walk up to upper management and talk about an idea.

But as Apple became a major corporation, the board decided it was time they grew up and got serious. They didn't understand the value of the cluster, so they got rid of Steve Jobs and hired in a top manager from Pepsi. Cola is a pretty static technology, so the new guy brought a ladder hierarchy. He didn't think what this would mean. He imposed 'order' and a firm chain of command: upper management got parking spaces and perks and cash incentives that the rest of the staff didn't get, creating a sudden gap between high and low.

Apple's productivity plummeted. It could not thrive with that kind of system. After a few years the guy from Pepsi was let go and Steve Jobs was brought back to restore the egalitarian style and get the company back on track.

Stereotypes

It can be tempting to stereotype men and women into chimpanzee roles, but in humans there's a great deal of cross-over. There are fiercely competitive ultra-feminine types who continually track who's thinner, who's richer and who's sporting the biggest diamond. They can also do damage if dropped into a cluster. Meanwhile, many modern males like Steve Jobs do open, egalitarian leadership; they just don't make Rambo movies or pick up nick-names like Neutron Jack.

For instance, Joel Barker is a world-renowned expert on paradigms, the search for industry-changing ideas. He's a true cluster Alpha: he's at the top of his field through respect, not intimidation; he's kind, even deferential to those of lower status and surprisingly inclusive of newcomers. This is not the kind of Alpha you'd expect at GE, yet he is perfectly suited to a rapidly changing field with an absolute premium on sharing information.

A cluster Alpha in an unexpected field is Ian Woodward, the stock investment guru. Stock investing is a macho business, with a good deal of bravado and posturing. Professional stock investors seem to delight in punching holes in each other's accomplishments. Woodward does none of this. He's an Alpha from his merit and the respect of his adherents, with a manner marked by patience, forbearance and even courtliness. Interestingly, this attitude communicates to the bulk of his followers who have created an egalitarian pocket in an otherwise cutthroat field.

One advantage of males who choose the cluster approach is that they seem more aware of the hazards of the pecking order, and know better how to handle such a person who comes to their world. Joel Barker is clear on the rules of fair play when it comes to new ideas. Ian Woodward is firm when members of his group will not stop taking shots at each other. Astute women managers also have this clarity and ability to set effective limits for the good of the group.

Inclusion/Exclusion

The cluster hierarchy puts a high value on inclusion; this is normally good solid care-taking, but like many good things it can go too far. Someone who is acting out may be catered to, so as not to upset them; someone who isn't quite competent may be protected, even when it puts a strain on the group. A cluster may try for agreement if not consensus in all decisions, or feel it ought to invite everyone to every meeting. This may be 'nice' but it may not be healthy. As with anything, inclusion needs to be balanced with sense and good judgment.

Sometimes a cluster will even include its opponents; if done wisely, this can work. Once, when Frances Hesselbein was head of the Girl Scouts, the organization was forced to sell some wilderness land and a group of protestors came to picket headquarters. It was a muggy, hot day in Manhattan, and so Hesselbein gave instructions to senior managers that they were to look after "our demonstrators" and ask them in for discussion over iced tea and cookies.

This didn't mean the Girl Scouts meant to capitulate, but it did mean they cared about the demonstrators and respected their concerns. Well, the protesters were upset individuals who clearly cared about similar values; what an excellent way to approach them. A ladder hierarchy would be more inclined to bar the door and pour hot oil from the towers.

Healthy and Unhealthy

The ladder system is not inevitably worse than the cluster; both have their uses. Both systems do healthy behavior when the hierarchy is stable and things are working well. Both will cross to unhealthy conflict if the system goes haywire.

A well-run, disciplined military team is an example of a ladder doing healthy, problem-solving behavior. It carries out its tasks with well-oiled efficiency and a pursuit of excellence. A deeply unhealthy military team becomes the U.S. Air Force Academy, displaying an outward show of excellence while secretly preying on its own members. Widespread rapes are not mere power plays or blind behavior, but outright tyranny and predation. A problem that bad isn't just due to a rigid structure. It's not the ladder per se that caused the breakdown, but the collapse of standards and power gone out of control.

In a different way, NASA was another ladder group gone haywire. Some engineers knew there was a problem with the shuttle craft, but higher ranking managers ignored them. The ladder was too locked into the pecking order to share information and it sacrificed members in a different way.

Clusters are prey to different sorts of breakdowns. For instance, a cluster isn't as accustomed to fighting and when it starts it may not stop. Think of the ladies in the church basement. If they work together well their group may be delightful, but if they start bickering they can make enemies that last twenty years. They may not have learned the value of putting their feelings aside and moving on for the good of the group.

In the ladder system people learn how to fight, but also they learn how to stop fighting. They can turn it on and off. This has its advantages. Two lawyers may battle it out in court, go have a pleasant lunch together, then come back to court to battle again. It's protocol, they don't bear a grudge. They know when to start and stop.

Perhaps neither of these systems is entirely suited to modern human society; the most successful structures seem to be hybrids. The ladders system gains by becoming more egalitarian and more open to sharing knowledge, while the cluster system benefits from firm limits and the ability to stop fighting. But members of both types of structures need to be aware of their strengths and weaknesses, because both of these systems will be around for a while.

What to Remember

In Ladder Hierarchies:

- **Dominance is enforced from the top down:** the Alpha gets to intimidate the Beta, the Beta gets to intimidate the Gamma, and so on.
- **Dominance may be enforced by aggression** and threat.
- **Higher ranks may resist** the advancement of the lower ranks.
- **Knowledge is the mark of the elite** and not to be shared.
- **When someone first enters** the hierarchy a hazing process will take place.

In Cluster Hierarchies:

- **The structure is arranged in banks of peers.** One Beta is not more Beta than the next.
- **The structure is held in place from the bottom up:** The Gammas defer to the Betas and everyone defers to the Alpha.
- **Care-taking** and personal gestures are important.
- **Knowledge is shared** readily.
- **Members may advance freely** through merit.

Overall:

- **Much of the problem comes from not recognizing different systems** and understanding their needs. A ladder hierarchy—like an airplane—needs a dose of egalitarianism so the Alpha can at least hear someone alerting him or her to a problem.
- **A cluster hierarchy**, which prides itself on inclusiveness, needs to know when to set limits especially if new members aren't playing by the rules.
- **A cluster hierarchy can benefit** from a layer of protection from the larger organization. It seems to thrive best in pockets, where the cluster is left in peace to do its cooperative thing.
- **Disaster can result** if an organization casually removes the cluster Alpha. Sometimes 'soft' leadership is the most effective kind.

What Works Where

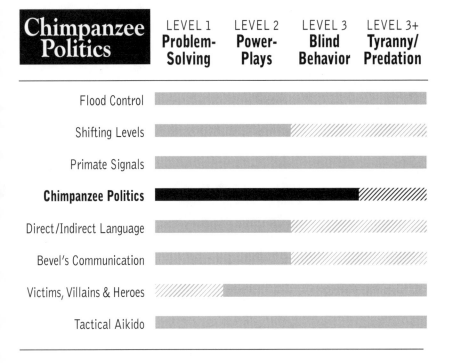

Chimpanzee Politics	LEVEL 1 Problem-Solving	LEVEL 2 Power-Plays	LEVEL 3 Blind Behavior	LEVEL 3+ Tyranny/Predation
Flood Control				
Shifting Levels				
Primate Signals				
Chimpanzee Politics				
Direct/Indirect Language				
Bevel's Communication				
Victims, Villains & Heroes				
Tactical Aikido				

Primate Politics cause complications that result in low-to mid-level conflict, but not the highest levels of conflict. For instance, the rapes at the Air Force Academy stem from prejudice and a predatory abuse of power; the ladder alone didn't cause it and adjusting the ladder won't fix it. But working with hierarchies can deliver good results in all categories short of outright tyranny.

Chapter Six

Communication Breakdowns: Direct and Indirect Language

Language alone, one would expect, couldn't cause many conflicts. Two people talk as they do every day; both speak English, more or less. If they have no reason to fight and face no undercurrents, why would they end up in conflict? But often infuriating problems are caused by nothing more involved than direct and indirect language.

Deborah Tannen is the linguist who popularized her arcane field for the general public. (Why linguists should have such trouble communicating is surely worth a study in itself.) However, Tannen pointed out that linguists had found there isn't one but *two* forms of English: direct and indirect language. In direct language, you say what you mean, no more, no less. In indirect language, you imply what you mean and assume the listener will read between the lines. This slight difference can lead to chaos.

Directs communicate well with directs. Indirects do well with indirects. Put a direct and an indirect together and they can antagonize each other in minutes.

The following is a conversation between an indirect and a direct:

INDIRECT: "Hi Jane. How's that project?"
(*Statement: "I need the work. Is it done yet?"*)
DIRECT: "It's getting along."
(*Interpretation: "I'll get around to it when I'm good and ready."*)
INDIRECT: "Well, do you think you're going to have it done soon?"
(*Statement: "Look, you can't act like this. Tell me when you'll have things ready."*)
DIRECT: "Yeah, probably."
(*Interpretation: "Don't push. I don't have to bother with you."*)

INDIRECT: "You know the project is really important."
(Statement: "I'm serious. I want some cooperation out of you.")
DIRECT: *(Confused)* "Well, yeah it's important. Who says it isn't?"
(Interpretation: "I'll play wounded dignity. You're just a jerk.")
INDIRECT: "Well, you sure don't act like it's important."
DIRECT: *(Offended)* "I don't act like it? What is wrong with you?"
INDIRECT: "What's wrong with me? You're the one who doesn't give a damn about this job!"

The fight is on.

Reading this, most people have one of two reactions: 1) This is ridiculous. Anyone could understand that. Or 2) This is absurd. No one could expect to do that kind of mind-reading.

Therein lies the problem. Indirect people find this conversation stupid and infuriating, an obvious example of passive-aggressive game-playing. Direct people find this same conversation murky and bizarre. Since neither can imagine trouble with the words themselves, they attribute the problem to plain stubborn meanness.

Indirect people tend to view directs as rude, boorish, antagonistic, insensitive, obnoxious and insubordinate. Indirects see directs as the proverbial bulls in the china shop, smashing things up by sheer careless ignorance. Indirects believe directs could do better but like to play stupid, refusing to understand a clear request or even a command.

Meanwhile, direct people tend to view indirects as evasive, manipulative, dishonest, sneaky, arbitrary, bad-tempered and temperamental. After all, they're always taking offense at nothing then going off to sulk. Directs believe indirects willfully withhold information, making the directs jump through hoops in a miserable, futile guessing game. They think it's done to torture them.

Here's an example between a couple:

INDIRECT: "Did you check out this garden walk in the newspaper?"
(Statement: "I want to go. Do you want to go, too?")
DIRECT: "Didn't look like much to me."
(Interpretation: "That's stupid. Stay home.")

INDIRECT: "Well, I think it could be very nice."
(*Meaning: "I want to go. You have no right to tell me not to."*)
DIRECT: "Do you really think so?"
(*Interpretation: "Really, really stupid."*)
INDIRECT: "Well, I'm going to look into it."
(*Meaning: "You have no right to treat me like this. I defy you."*)
DIRECT: "Fine. Have a good time."
(*Interpretation: "Be an idiot if you want to."*)
INDIRECT: "Well, I will have a good time."
(*Meaning: "I intend to stand up for my rights."*)
DIRECT: "What is your problem? Why are you acting like this?"
(*Interpretation: Direct onslaught. The fight is on.*)

Psychologists in this country tend to disapprove of indirect speech, considering it unhealthy and manipulative. Linguists, however, disagree: they insist indirect speech is a valid communication style, and they've studied this in detail. It may not be what direct types expect, but it certainly communicates once you know the rules.

Indirects usually understand each other well, although the conversation can be mystifying to a direct speaker. The following is a negotiation between two indirects:

Phil walks into the office with a radio:

PHIL: "Hi Jane. Are you still working that report?"
(*Question: Can I turn on the radio and listen to the ballgame?*)
JANE: "Yep." (*Answer: No.*)
PHIL: "How's the report going?" (*Question: Pretty please?*)
JANE: It's really rough, but I'm hanging in there. (*Answer: Forget it.*)

A direct person would not have the slightest idea what was going on, and in fact, if the World Series was on, he might walk over and turn on the radio himself. And he'd have no idea why Jane would stomp out the office and glower at him for the rest of the week.

Context

Indirect language makes use of context. For instance, Phil walked into the office with a radio in his hands. That's an important signal and sets the tone for everything that follows.

Direct speakers rely on words, not context. They say, "I'd like to listen to the game. Do you mind?" It won't matter if they're holding a radio or a rhinoceros. The exception would be if the direct were deliberately making a point, such as saying "I want to listen to that game," while holding a .38 automatic. Even a direct speaker would get the point.

Directs are quite overt. If the other person hasn't said things in so many words, they won't get it.

I once explained this material and looked over to see one woman, Alexandra, holding her head in her hands. When I asked what was wrong, she told the following story.

Alexandra worked at a company with a woman who was also a neighbor. They both had small children and both used the company day care center.

The day before the workshop, Alexandra got a call from her neighbor in the middle of the afternoon saying, "I'm really swamped over here. It looks like I may end up working overtime tonight."

"Yes?" said Alexandra.

"I mean, we're short-staffed and it looks like I could be here 'till seven. I've still got two reports that have to go out tonight. "

"Really?" said Alexandra. "That's a lot."

The conversation went on like this for several minutes, with the neighbor explaining how swamped she was and Alexandra nodding sympathetically. After a while, the neighbor hung up, and Alexandra did not think anything more about it.

That evening Alexandra noticed her neighbor was furious.

What was that all about?

A) The neighbor was a real whiner.

B) Alexandra was a clod.

C) The neighbor wanted Alexandra to pick up her kid from the day care center and keep him with the other kids until the neighbor could get home from work.

The answer, of course, is C. Was any of this mentioned in the conversation? Not a word of it. The meaning came from context. The only things Alexandra and the neighbor had in common were the company, their kids and the day care center. They didn't talk about anything else. Since Alexandra didn't respond, it was the indirect equivalent of saying, "I'm not going to help you. Tough."

This neighbor had covered for Alexandra any number of times and Alexandra owed her the favor. Alexandra didn't have the faintest idea that she had offended her neighbor or let her down. But therein lies the usefulness. Once Alexandra apologized and explained, the fight was over. Alexandra meant no disrespect and she made it clear she'd help in the future. She just needed some more verbal cues.

Requests

Like neighbor who wanted help with day care, people get especially indirect about requests. Indirects find it hard to ask for a favor in so many words. They feel a direct request is an imposition. It puts the other person in the position of possibly having to say "No," which is rude and embarrassing for everyone involved.

Instead, indirect speakers skirt the problem by gently implying what they want. That way neither side needs to lose face if the answer is no. This approach gets used even if the request is one that no one would refuse.

A couple was driving cross-country. The boyfriend, who was driving, spoke direct while the girlfriend spoke indirect. The girlfriend wanted to stop for a bathroom. A rest stop appeared ahead, and, being indirect, she asked the driver, "Do you want to stop here?" The boyfriend considered it a moment and said, "I don't think so," and kept driving.

The girlfriend was dumbfounded. How could anyone be so rude? Besides, it was her car! She fumed, and soon there was an exit with some restaurants. She asked, "Would you like to stop at one of these places?" The boyfriend eyed the fast food dives and said, "No, not really," and drove past.

By now the girlfriend was furious. Another exit came up and she said, "Why don't you stop here. I want to use the bathroom." The boyfriend said, "OK," and pulled off at the stop. As his girlfriend stormed off he had some idea that something was wrong, but he couldn't imagine what it was.

How could he have offended her? They hadn't even talked. All he had done was drive the car.

The girlfriend was further offended at the way her boyfriend pretended not to know what was wrong. She considered it passive-aggressive game-playing of the worst order.

To be fair, direct speakers do sometimes get the hint, and they refuse to acknowledge it because they resent the hinting around. They feel the whole business is manipulative. They feel if someone wants something, they should be frank and say so instead of dodging around.

Directs tend not to see anything explosive about requests. Directs are fairly comfortable with saying "No," although that is often the last thing on their minds. But they can't say "No" until they hear the request in the first place. Directs have no idea how many requests they refuse.

Indirects tend to see conversation as something of a minefield; people could be offended at any point, so it's wise to tread lightly so that doesn't happen. Directs just see conversation as so many words. Since they don't expect trouble they just plod along, setting off explosions left and right.

Indirects feel that only an idiot would plod across a minefield in a straight line. Since the direct person clearly isn't an idiot, they must like making trouble. And then they have the audacity to play the wounded innocent after they caused all the damage.

Yes and No

Which of the following is an indirect's way of saying, "No"?

A) I'll have to see about it.
B) Can I get back to you on this?
C) I don't know.
D) All of the above.

The answer is D, All of the above. Refusing a request is a potentially rude thing to do, and indirects hate to say anything as crude as, "No." Direct speakers desperately wish they would.

When direct speakers hear, "I'll get back to you on that," they patiently wait for the return phone call. They feel foolish and insulted when they discover that the other person never meant to call back and the answer was "No," all along.

Direct speakers don't have the same trouble with "No." They consider it a nice, short word that covers everything they need to know. Of course they'd prefer "Yes," but "No" is something they can live with.

Which of the following is a direct speaker's way of saying "No?"

A) No.
B) I don't think so.
C) I won't be able to do it, but why don't you ask Mac?
D) All of the above.

The answer, of course, is all of the above. The problem is that all but C will be considered rude. Indirects are no more devastated by refusal than anyone else; they just prefer it to be couched in a different way. Indirects may pad the sentence, adding more words, phrasing things in a roundabout manner. Unfortunately, indirects can be so circumspect about "No" that the direct may have no idea what's going on.

A manager was taking in program ideas from the community, when an elderly man came to her with a suggestion. She was direct, he was indirect. He explained his idea and looked hopefully at the manager. She couldn't figure out what he was talking about. He tentatively explained again. They did a few rounds of this. Bewildered, she said, "I have to tell you that I don't know what to make of it. Why do you want to do this program?"

The elderly man was crushed. In indirect that meant "That was really stupid." She had no idea she had hurt his feelings. Besides she still didn't know what he had in mind.

In a situation like this, it sometimes helps to use paper and pencil. Tactfully explain your confusion: "I seem to be having trouble getting a grip on this. Now, I tend to think in bullet points. Could you help me map this out?"

Indirects can be much more forward sketching ideas on paper or filling out a chart. Only so many words fit in the box, and they'll have no trouble with that.

In some cultures it's simply not acceptable to say, "No." An American traveling in Asia stopped in a small shop in Hong Kong to replace her battered notebook. She held up her small, black, leather-bound pad and said, "Do you have a notebook like this?"

The clerk looked around the store and brought out a spiral-bound paper book and said, "We have a notebook like this." The American said, "No, I need a notebook like this." The clerk looked around again, and held up a large portfolio and said, "We have a notebook like this." She kept going around and around in the store, holding up objects that were nothing like a small black leather notebook. Finally the American said, "So what you're saying is, you don't have a notebook like this." The clerk said, "Yes!" visibly relieved.

"No" can be a touchy business in families, even among direct folk. For instance, people have all sorts of ways of saying they don't want to be disturbed. Often, it can be easier to keep the peace if you don't actually say the words "No," or "Go away." ("Please go away" doesn't make it any better.) Hard feelings can be avoided by using a signal.

Becky was an artist in a crowded household. When she was drawing she wanted to be left alone, which was always going to upset someone. So she hit on the idea of wearing her engineer's hat. The message was clear: if Becky was wearing her engineer's hat, she was drawing and wanted to be left alone. Everyone was fine with that.

When Directs Get Indirect

Directs can get pretty huffy about all this, but as one indirect pointed out, everyone gets indirect sometime. Let's say you've been invited to a party at the home of your new boss. You don't know him well and you've never met his family. In the midst of the party you go to the ice chest to look for ice, and there isn't any.

Do you:

A) Yell, "Hey! You're outta ice!"

B) Call, "Want me to get some ice? You're out."

C) Quietly close the ice chest, go back to your host and say, "Do you have any ice?" Then let your boss lead you back to the ice chest, let him open it up and let *him* discover that there is no ice. Then he can show you where there's extra ice, or you can offer to make a run to the store.

C is indirect, but that's how most people would handle the situation (except for those who would quietly do without). It isn't how you would handle the situation around your best friend, or with your brother-in-law and his poker buddies. But you know those people and they're not your boss.

Courtesy and Rudeness

Americans can be suspicious of indirect language, but other cultures see it as the norm. For instance, the British middle-class is raised on indirectness as common courtesy. In Japan and many parts of Asia, it's required.

Indirect people often speak this way because they were raised to do so and because it's their way of being polite. They would no more blurt out an order or a criticism than they would put their feet on the dinner table.

Direct people show courtesy in a different way. For them, courtesy demands they say, "Please," and "Thank you." That covers it.

To most indirects, that's quite rude. One program director was astonished at the very suggestion. "Are you telling me," she asked, "that when I need Jack to meet a deadline, I should just march in, throw the papers on his desk and say, 'Here's the stuff, Jack. I need it Tuesday.' Are you out of your mind?"

Jack was sitting across the room, and he said, "Yes, that's what I want. Because then I would actually know what you wanted and I wouldn't have to guess."

The manager was incredulous. But Jack didn't see it as rude, he saw it as the end to the guessing game. Then some other indirect managers started explaining how indirect language was so much more polite. A direct subordinate calmly replied, "That's not polite. It makes you want to strangle them." The indirects were rather taken aback, but it did make the point. In direct fashion.

Unintentional Warfare

Cynthia was a black working class woman who spoke direct English. She had a white graduate school professor, who spoke indirect English, at an upper class college where most people spoke indirect. Cynthia was trying to get along with these people, who seemed maddeningly vague.

The professor was uncomfortable with Cynthia's direct statements in class, like "I wouldn't do it that way at all," or "Sounds like nothing but trouble." The other indirects didn't take this as discussion; they took it as confrontation and they'd stop talking.

Talking with Cynthia in his office, the professor vaguely mentioned conversations in class. Cynthia wanted to get this right, so she put her cards on the table in direct fashion: "I'm trying to get along here. What is it you want me to do?"

The professor, stung, said, "It would be nice if other people could have a chance to be heard."

"Does that mean you want me to shut up?"

"We need to encourage an open discussion."

"I feel that way, too, but you haven't answered my question."

"What question?"

"Do you want me to talk less? I don't care if I do, I just want to know what it is that you want. Is that it?"

"Why don't you try that?"

Having finally gotten something like clear orders, Cynthia sat through the next class and didn't say a word. Finally the professor asked if she didn't have anything to say. She replied, in front of the entire class, "Well, you told me not to talk. What do you want?"

Cynthia reported that her professor went quite pale. To an indirect person, Cynthia had not only jettisoned the compromise, she had ambushed him in public and was one step short of a discrimination suit.

None of this, of course, was what Cynthia intended. She was

trying to get along. To Cynthia, the professor was being unreasonable and contradictory; she was following his directions and now he wanted something else. And from that point the professor studiously avoided her. He would not meet with her in private, but she did come away with a good grade.

Complementary Breakdown

Both Cynthia and the professor were trying to solve the problem, and they were doing it the only way they knew how. By doing the reasonable, natural, helpful thing they were making life impossible for each other.

Gregory Bateson was an anthropologist, and he came up with a name for this: complementary schizogenesis. That is, complementary—both sides working together; schizo—division or rift, as in schism; and genesis—to create. It means both sides are working together to create a division, even while they're trying to patch things up.

The easiest way to picture this is a practical joke with an electric blanket that has dual controls. One person likes to sleep warm, and the other likes to sleep cool. But now a joker switches the controls.

Since he likes it warm, one sleeper sets the dial to seven, which means *her* side of the bed heats up. Since her side is warm, she dials down to four, which cools down *his* side of the bed. Since he's getting colder, he sets his up to eight—which cools down her side, so she dials down to two, so he pushes his to nine, and so on until they are both ready to rip the dials off the cord.

This is exactly what happens with direct and indirect language. The indirect speaker senses a problem, and does his best to smooth things over by being tactfully indirect. The direct speaker also feels the tension, so he tries to fix it in the only sensible way: by being frank and to the point. The more blunt the direct speaker is, the more vague the indirect speaker becomes until they both want to flee the room.

The common cure for the schizogenesis is to abruptly hit reverse:

do the opposite of whatever it was you were just doing. If you were being blunt, stop, use more words and get oblique. If you were being tactfully indirect, try a blunt sentence and see if it works. If it's a schizogenesis, you'll immediately sense relief when you do the reverse.

The schizogenesis can work in all sorts of ways. I do most of my work in isolation and expect phone calls only in emergencies. I was working with a new client who was very social and chatty. After our first meeting, the client called me up the next day to touch base. I picked up the phone thinking, "What? What's wrong? What could have gone wrong so soon?" She chatted a little about this and that, and pretty soon got off the phone. I couldn't for the life of me understand the point.

We both had the unsettling feeling that something was wrong. Wanting to clear things up, she called me back, which only startled me more, so I got off the phone. Wanting to set things straight, she called me up again and again. The more she called, the more abrupt I got, so the more she called to make the peace. It got to the point she was calling four and five calls a day. I was getting frantic.

Finally I realized that we had a schizogenesis going on, and I abruptly hit reverse. First thing the next morning, I called *her*. We chatted a little and got off the phone. That was the end of it. She stopped calling. To her, my phone call meant all was well, so she could finally stop calling.

This kind of thing is likely to come up if you're dealing with someone from another culture, ethnicity, background or gender. Take, for instance, New Yorkers and Midwesterners. New Yorkers sometimes will try to be friendly by insulting people. Think Seinfeldt. A rude joke can mean that they really like you. Midwesterners tend to be much more low-key. They don't see insults as a social skill, especially not with people they don't know well.

The New Yorker who wants to make friends may get abrasive. The Midwesterner, trying to coexist, will get more withdrawn. So the New

Yorker tries harder and prods the Midwesterner, and the Midwestern pulls into his shell. Like a kid with a turtle, the New Yorker pokes harder to get the Midwesterner to come out and play. Each one is trying to co-exist and yet they're just provoking each other.

A New Yorker once asked me, "What does it take to get along with these people? I feel like I'm practically ostracized around here." And the Midwesterners pulled me aside to say, "Can you get him to stuff a sock in it? Please?"

Sometimes it helps to signal that you mean well, since others have no way of knowing that you do. You can say, "You know, I'm a Brooklyn kind of guy. If I say something wrong, put my foot in my mouth, just pour a cup of coffee on my head. Just so I know I've done it again." An indirect might say, "You know, sometimes I try to be so careful that I'm not always sure I get my point across. So if I've get too obscure just let me know, and I'll see if I can cut to the chase."

Half the time, all people want is some plausible way of dealing with you. Signal that you mean well, then give them some pointers on how to proceed. They probably mean no harm; they just want to know how to get past this.

But it's Wrong, Wrong, Wrong

There is no right or wrong here. Direct language is not better or more honest than indirect, and indirect language is not inherently more intelligent or sophisticated than direct. Both forms of English exist; neither one will go away. No one is going to grow out of this. There is nothing left to do but cope.

This is one of the costs of having such a diverse country. If we were all Japanese we wouldn't be having this trouble. But we're not. We come from all sorts of different backgrounds and different cultures treat this different ways.

Of course, one of the interesting things about all this is that people tend to marry someone who speaks the opposite way. This makes for some splendid family fights and a good many divorces.

Solving the Problem

What can be done about all this?

The first step in solving the problem is to simply realize that there is such a language difference, that it's common, and to watch for it. It's likely to keep happening with the same people. Don't let the frustration drive you into level two. Don't flood, stay calm, go back to problem-solving.

Those who speak direct can learn to pick up on indirect language and hear when things are going out of whack. However, direct people almost never learn to speak indirect. They might patch together a sentence or two, but I've yet to see a direct speaker become fluent in indirect. The nuances are too subtle and, for a direct person, too obscure.

Instead, if you're direct, try to speak intentionally gently, the way you'd speak to your grandmother. Around an elder you might cushion the phrase a little, wrap some more words around it. You wouldn't say, "Grandma, don't you know better?" You'd say, "Wait a minute, Grandma. Are you sure this is what you want to do?" This isn't being patronizing, it's using a different style of speech.

Speaking to an indirect, phrase statements as questions, especially loaded statements. Direct: "That was dumb." Indirect: "Is this the only way we can do this?" You have to admit, indirect is a lot more diplomatic.

Finally, if you're direct find an indirect friend who's willing to be your translator. Use this person from time to time before you send off business letters. It could save you a lot of grief.

If you're an indirect speaker, learn to take direct people at face value however strange that may seem. Understand that people may be willing to cooperate with you, but can't understand what you want. Try being more blunt, even though it feels rude. Not only will direct people not be offended, they will be relieved.

If you're starting from misunderstanding, it generally does *not* pay to keep explaining yourself over and over. You can get bogged down in "What I meant," and "What I heard you hear me say…" Since you're using different language to start with, talking more tends to compound the problem. For instance, if you keep trying to make an indirect person clarify himself, he's likely to think you're trying to box him into a corner, trying to pin him down. In indirect, that's a form of fighting. He'll become more evasive, not less.

Quit while you're ahead. You understand, so make the corrections and go on with things. If this is a person you are particularly close to (such as someone you wake up to in the morning), just hand over the chapter.

What to Remember

Handling language breakdowns is a fundamental skill; you can't solve a problem if the other side can't fathom what you're talking about. Of course you'd prefer that the other side spoke your way, but as Bevel might point out, it does no good to wait until someone else can understand you. These aren't deep-rooted problems, so you may as well get them out of the way.

FOR DIRECT SPEAKERS: understanding an Indirect

- If a conversation does not make sense stop and listen for indirect meanings.
- If a conversation suddenly feels hostile check for indirect meanings.
- Do not try to 'pin down' the indirect by asking blunt questions. In indirect language, that's a form of fighting.
- If, at last resort, you cannot fathom what the other person is trying to communicate, say the direct opposite and wait to be corrected.

FOR DIRECT SPEAKERS: speaking to an Indirect

- Phrase your statements in a gentler manner.
- Use more words to 'pad' your statements.
- Phrase loaded statements as questions: i.e., instead of, "I think we should..." say, "Do you think we might..."
- If the speaker becomes more vague or indirect, become more indirect yourself.
- Ask the indirect speaker to use bullet points, or sketch the idea in a chart.

FOR INDIRECT SPEAKERS: understanding an Direct

- Take all statements at face value: nothing more, nothing less.
- "Please" and "Thank you" are to be taken literally.
- Do not become offended unless you are quite sure that offense is intended.
- Verbal 'land mines' will be clearly marked.

FOR INDIRECTS: speaking to a Direct

- If the listener doesn't understand you, shorten your sentences. Get specific.
- If you get an inappropriate response, say your most important point and then stop.
- Adjust your sense of courtesy. To a direct speaker, blunt statements won't be viewed as rude. They'll like it.

What Works Where

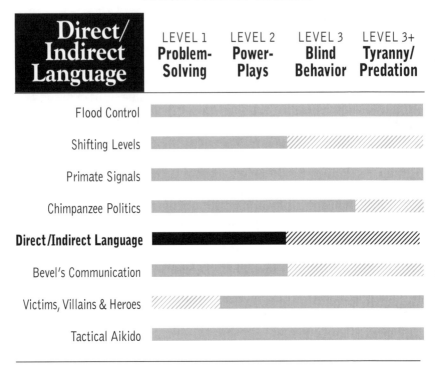

Direct/ Indirect Language	LEVEL 1 Problem- Solving	LEVEL 2 Power- Plays	LEVEL 3 Blind Behavior	LEVEL 3+ Tyranny/ Predation
Flood Control				
Shifting Levels				
Primate Signals				
Chimpanzee Politics				
Direct/Indirect Language				
Bevel's Communication				
Victims, Villains & Heroes				
Tactical Aikido				

Direct/Indirect Language can easily cause lower level conflicts. Of course, language gaffs can turn up at any time, but they are primarily found at levels one or two.

Chapter Seven

Solving Problems with Finesse: The Principle of Communciation

After a presentation a young man, Phillip Bradley, took me aside to tell me about some conflict techniques he used in working with gangs and community kids on the south side of Chicago. His mentor was the Rev. James Bevel, who had been a strategist for Dr. Martin Luther King.

Bevel was one of the more eccentric and controversial of the civil rights leaders. Possessed of a dazzlingly quick mind, he was capable of generating hundreds if not thousands of ideas, some of which were openly contradictory of each other. Many researchers found Bevel so trying they dismissed his modern work. But Phillip Bradley seems to have captured the best of Bevel; I like to think the concepts in this book present Bevel at his finest.

The following technique is remarkably effective at levels one or two; however, it fails outright by level three. But more on that later.

Non-violence as a whole has been an overlooked lode of material. Conflict specialists are more likely to draw on law or family counseling, even the martial arts and tactical warfare. Non-violence is regarded as a noble philosophy, all very 'evolved,' but not a source of serious tactics. But think about it: in most situations you don't want dead bodies on the floor. Cutthroat tactics sound impressive, but the results are messy and hard to live with. Non-violence provides ingenious alternatives.

Non-violence is also overlooked because these tactics are assumed to come from a position of weakness. The assumption seems to be that if you had real strength you'd use force; yet all great strategists came from a position of weakness. Napoleon, Robert E. Lee, Chief Joseph, the great minds studied at the War College all came from a position of weakness. If they had overwhelming force at their disposal, they wouldn't have needed great strategy.

Bevel was not only tactically brilliant, he was able to reduce sophisticated techniques into simple procedures that anyone could follow.

This is his Principle of Communication, and it's not much to look at. It has only three short steps:

1) Ask the right question.
2) Listen to the answer.
3) Have the courage to act on what you hear.

Nothing to it, right? Watch how it plays.

A manager had an employee who wouldn't take direction—just wouldn't listen. The manager went over to his office to pass along the message that he was to call back a client. Instead of just saying, "OK," the employee gave him a lot of excuses why that wasn't possible. Flooding, the manager burst out, "Just call the damn guy," and stormed off. As he slammed out he walked into his own boss coming down the hall.

Cooling down, the manager thought that perhaps this wasn't a shining example of management technique, and he thought about how he might do better. He'd already tried everything else he could think of, so he decided to try Bevel.

Over lunch the manager asked the employee why he wouldn't take suggestions. The employee looked a little uncomfortable, shifted in his chair, and pointed out that the boss actually had asked him that question before.

Well. The manager had to admit that they did have this conversation before, but he couldn't for the life of him remember what was said. So this time he promised to listen.

The employee explained that he knew the manager was older and more experienced, but felt that he talked down to him at times. He'd really prefer it if the manager would ask him what he thought before telling him what to do. If the employee wanted to try it his own way first, he'd like the manager to give him the benefit of the doubt and let him try. If things didn't work out he'd do it the manager's way, but he wanted to try his own way first.

Having listened, the manager now had to have the courage to act on what he heard. He decided to give it a try.

In turn, the employee admitted that he was too stubborn and asked the manager to remind him if he were getting rigid again. They shook on it and had a working deal.

Looking for an Answer

Being intelligent people, when faced with a conflict we naturally search for an answer. But in doing that we overlook an obvious source: the other person.

We get used to looking at the other side as the source of the problem, an obstacle, something to outwit. We fail to notice that these people may actually know what could end the problem. As the other half of the conflict they may hold the other half of the information, and if we ask them in a civil manner they just might tell us.

It may also be true that the other side has been trying to tell us the same information for months, if not years.

For instance, your staff may have said repeatedly, "Stop calling meetings. Your meetings are making us crazy. We can never get anything done because we always have to go to more meetings."

Your job at this point is not to defend your stance on meetings or to clarify once again how important meetings are. Remember, you've already been through this seventy times. Your job is to listen. If you like, you can ask more questions, such as:

"OK, if we don't do meetings, how can I stay informed on the project?"

Listen to the answer, then have the courage to act on what you hear. Showing courage does not mean automatically agreeing with whatever you hear. That's capitulation. Courage means responding appropriately. You may think it over and come back with a counteroffer: "Right now we're doing eight meetings a month. What if we reduce it to four meetings? At the end of the month we can re-evaluate and see how things are going."

No one said it would be easy to listen to what people have to say. If it was easy, it wouldn't require courage. People may tell you, "Things are going great, J.B., couldn't be better." This may be the most ominous statement of all, because it means that people think it's best to lie to you and feel confident to do so.

Courage

People often think they show courage by ignoring what they hear. "You think I'm going to pay attention to garbage like that? Of course not!" People act as if stonewalling is a show of strength. In fact, it's a show of weakness. Any ninny can refuse to hear; it takes no skill, no I.Q. and no judgment. People with no sense rely on this tactic all the time.

This false show of strength can sometimes be disastrous. The most shocking revelation from the secret tapes of Lyndon Johnson was that Johnson himself believed the War in Viet Nam was unwinnable and knew that from the beginning of his presidency.

We lost 45,000 Americans in Viet Nam, with far more Vietnamese killed. Protestors rioted across the country while asserting that Americans had no business in that war, and now we learn that Johnson privately agreed. The problem was that he couldn't admit he agreed. He thought anti-war demonstrators were communist inspired and that he would look weak to admit they were right. So he continued to commit more soldiers to a cause that he knew was doomed to fail.

It would have taken courage to admit the administration had made a mistake and Johnson's courage failed him. The war in Vietnam destroyed his presidency and damaged a generation. In the end, both

Johnson and the demonstrators were proved right: the war couldn't be won, at least not by arms.

Listening, and acting on what you hear, is not for the faint-hearted. You might have to hear that your next in command, the one you were grooming to take over, is a charming slacker. You may have to hear that your own priceless child has been getting away with murder because her parents think she's a darling angel. You may need to hear that your favorite project needs to be euthanized or at least undergo major surgery. Perhaps the scariest statement of all is: "We'd like you to trust our judgment." You'll have to decide if that is a good plan, or how you can make it a good plan. The courage to act, after all, is not merely being a rubberstamp or abdicating your own responsibility.

This technique will require your holding fast to problem-solving and doing your job as a professional, spouse or parent. You'll need to draw on the kind of courage and judgment that's only available at level one, not to mention the stoicism. Perhaps you'll get good news when you ask the right question, but you certainly can't count on it. That's where the courage comes in.

The Right Answer Is Not Necessarily the One You Want to Hear

One father was dealing with his carefully sheltered teenaged daughter who was away for her first year at college. The family was Muslim, and the daughter called from school to explain to Dad that her boyfriend would be driving up to visit—and staying in her dorm room.

Dad managed not to hit the ceiling but calmly explained, with admirable Dad reasoning, why this was not a good idea. Daughter calmly reasoned back that nothing would happen and there surely wouldn't be a problem. Getting nowhere at all, Dad finally put his foot down. Daughter promptly saw the light and told him he was right and would do exactly what he said.

The Dad was very proud when he described the story. Unfortunately, I had to explain that the likelihood was that his daughter had figured out the fastest way to shut him up was to tell him he was right. He'd been hustled.

This was quite a guy and he made this a personal project. He realized that his daughter was growing up and was just as smart as he was. He could no longer tell her what to do, even though she was achingly inexperienced in the realities of American dating. For him to maintain his influence, he had to shift from the Dad who told her what to do, to the Dad who could dialogue. This was important because, while his daughter was intelligent and confident, she still had a lot to learn about teenage boys.

The Lecture

This earnest, loving Dad had delivered The Lecture. Managers deliver The Lecture as well, laying down the law in a firm, just way. Teachers, even judges succumb to The Lecture.

The Lecture is a sad, glorious, useless thing. Sad because it represents so many of our dreams and aspirations that so seldom come right, the moment when we are Right, and the erring malefactor knows it and looks up at us, sadder but wiser. Glorious because we have justice, resolution and strength tempered with mercy, and we are doing our best—our well-spoken, deep-wisdom best—and the malefactor is there to see it and be swayed.

And it's useless because it's all just a hustle. They've got us scoped. They know exactly what we want to hear, and they're handing it to us on a plate.

I had to explain to this dad that his daughter hadn't heard a word he said. She knew the old man and had figured out that the easiest way to get rid of him was to sound impressed and agree.

Talking isn't the key to the solution—*listening* is. As long as the malefactors have us talking and grandstanding, they're off the hook. We'll talk ourselves out and be satisfied to boot. They don't have to do a thing but look up at us with soulful eyes. I once knew a Labrador retriever who could lay it on splendidly when he'd been caught chewing the rug, and that wasn't a particularly smart dog.

Dialogue

One of the keys to Bevel's technique is that it opens a dialogue. Normally, when faced with a problem we talk at the other person and try to get them to see things our way. That's different from talking *with* the other person. We start by going through all our telling points, and if the other person tries to get a word in we talk faster. Or maybe we're polite and hear them out, while actually we're thinking of what we'll say next.

That's not a dialogue. That's a monologue.

People hate sitting through a monologue. Needless to say, monologues are seldom successful, no matter how strong our arguments are. The simple fact of being talked at makes people not listen.

I've asked many people to describe how they feel while they're being talked at.

Then I asked them to describe their feelings while they're being talked *with*, that is, to engage in genuine give and take.

Here's the list:

Monologue	Dialogue
Miserable	Relief
Angry	Respected
Captured	Respectful
Railroaded	Scared
Simmering	Justified
Insulted	Curious
Helpless/Hopeless	Anger somehow tied with hope
Demeaned	Vulnerable
Devalued	Creative
Defensive	Confident
Provoked	A feeling of possibility
Embarrassed	Sometimes a feeling of exhilaration
Seething	Oddly comforted
Not caring/not being cared for	

It's hardly surprising that we don't get cooperation from someone who's feeling talked at. As angry as they are, how likely is it that this person is going to stay in the healthy end of the continuum? For that matter, what better way to boost morale but to defy us or ignore us completely?

We might go into a monologue meaning well and thinking we're being convincing. Actually, we're just being provoking.

Now consider the likelihood of finding cooperation somewhere within that second list. In fact, you could make worthless arguments and the second case would still be more likely to win cooperation—although that's not strictly a fair comparison, since the odds of cooperation resulting from the first list is nearly zero.

Part of the cooperation is because the second list describes someone who feels that they're being treated as an adult. The first list is all about being treated like a child, so you can hardly be surprised if you get a juvenile response.

This goes back to that old issue of respect and supply and demand. People who feel respected are far more likely to deal with you in a reasonable fashion. Listening is a way of showing respect, which is in short supply.

Like any other honor, listening must be done with sincerity. False or manipulative listening, like false or manipulative praise, is a serious betrayal and can earn you deep hostility.

Now, a lot of what passes for dialogue isn't the real thing. I once heard someone say, "I dialogue with my sister, but we're constantly interrupting each other." Well, if you're interrupting, that's not dialogue. That's a description of two simultaneous monologues.

Stopping the Spiral

The most common problem in conflict is getting pulled out of problem-solving into an unwanted power struggle. The principle of communication is very good at turning that around.

A graphic artist worked at a high-powered mutual funds company, where they would package stock bundles and present them to major buyers. These presentations had to be just so. The research was done by a band of young, fiercely competitive stock analysts who worked out of the company bullpen. Timing was crucial; the package had to go from final analysis to formal presentation within forty-eight hours.

The company was a macho place, and the artist was one of the few women there apart from the secretaries.

A young female analyst joined the bullpen, but she kept getting the presentations wrong. She would use the wrong formats, which threw a wrench into the works when there was no time for mistakes.

The artist went to the bullpen to talk to her about it and only got an argument. As the two of them went at it, the guys started jeering, "Meow. Meow." Realizing this was going nowhere, the artist walked out feeling out-numbered and humiliated.

This was bad. She had to get through to this analyst because she couldn't afford any more near-disasters. There had to be a better way, so she tried the Principle of Communication.

She got the analyst away from the bullpen to talk to her privately. She started by asking the question: "Why do you think we're having this problem?" And the analyst answered: "Because you don't like that I'm a woman."

Well, the analyst had it backwards—the artist liked that she was a woman. The artist felt there was far too much testosterone in that place, and if anyone was going to break the glass ceiling it would have to be the analyst. The artist couldn't do it; she would never make partner.

The more they talked the more it became clear that the analyst had no idea what was expected of her. The artist had her attention but still couldn't figure out just what was going wrong. Finally she hit the right question: "How much training did they give you on these presentations?" The answer: "Two hours." The company was supposed to provide two *days* worth of training on the presentation format. At the time they hired the analyst they were so short-handed they just grabbed her and threw her in the bullpen. She had no idea how these projects ought to be done, and her fiercely competitive colleagues certainly weren't going to tell her.

So that was it. The artist then went to the boss and explained that the presentation training hadn't happened. The analyst got the training she needed and the artist got an ally in the bullpen.

What's the Right Question?

Asking the right question is often a matter of trial and error. In the example above, the artist wrote up a list of questions before she walked in, which was wise. The situation itself may be so confusing—or upsetting—that you may not be able to think at the spur of the moment. You may start flooding and have your mind go blank.

Don't be surprised if your first question isn't the right question. Count on needing at least three questions.

Yes or no questions won't work. After all, you need to get this person talking, and yes/no questions can get you shut out. In the same way, rhetorical questions don't count. "Are you stupid, or what?" is not going to open a dialogue.

You can tell when you ask the right question because there will be a sudden spark in the air; their eyes change, the atmosphere goes electric. Abruptly everything changes.

One mom had two kids, an eight-year-old son by her first marriage and a three-year-old daughter by her present marriage. The son had stayed home from school for two days with a stomach ache. He wasn't running a fever and didn't seem to be sick, so Mom started wondering just what was going on. She decided to try Bevel.

"How are you getting along at school?"

"Fine."

"How are you getting along with your teacher?"

"Fine."

"How are you getting along with the other kids?"

"Fine."

Think, think, think. "How are you getting along with your sister?"

It was like a dam bursting. The kid couldn't get words out fast enough. It seems the problem was that his little sister was getting a lot more attention than he was. She was little and cute and everybody made a big deal over her. Nobody even noticed him any more.

He hauled his mom over to look in the closet. His sister had racks of cute little baby shoes. He had exactly two pairs.

Mom had never thought about how this must feel to her son. It's true, they were excited at having a baby girl, and it was a lot of fun to dress her up like a doll. Mom didn't think her son cared about shoes and, in fact, he didn't. He cared about getting forgotten.

Now Mom had to have the courage to act on what she heard. She was a busy working mom, but she carved out time to do special things with her son. She kept it just the two of them, so he could feel special, too.

Using this tactic with kids presents special problems, because kids don't necessarily know how to talk about what's really going on with them. That's a social skill that not many adults have mastered, so expect kids to need some extra effort.

Learning to talk about feelings is crucial for kids. Specialists who worked with violent kids found that the fastest way to change a kid from violent to not violent was to teach him or her how to talk about feelings. That worked better than spanking, punishment, shaming or even peer pressure. If kids could relieve their feelings by talking they didn't need to hit somebody; from there they could learn other social skills they needed to get along.

You've probably wondered how you can send your kid into the world protected and prepared. You may not be able to teach your kid to bat .500 or program a Unix network, but if you can teach your kid to talk about feelings you'll have given that kid an edge in life.

Talking with Teenagers

Teenagers present a different set of problems. They might be better able to talk, but they'll have a new set of reasons why they won't.

One mom was worried about her 16-year-old son, who'd been staying overnight at a friend's house. He hadn't been close to this kid before, and there had been rumors that the kid's parents were a little off-base. A lot of the kids had started staying over and the mom wanted to check it out.

She started out blunt: "What's going on over there? I want to know." That got her shut out immediately. The kid got sarcastic, Mom got mad, and they both veered into psychological warfare. Mom realized she was flooding and left the room for a while.

About a half hour later, she'd calmed down and approached him again. She apologized for losing her temper, and her son apologized for getting sarcastic. They were now both back at level one. So she tried another question: "Why is it the 'in' thing to stay over at that house?" Her son just put his head down and shrugged.

Getting a little more oblique, she asked, "Who else is going over there?" Her son mumbled a few names, then lapsed into silence.

Still trying to be roundabout , she asked, "Are the parents at home when the kids are over there?" Her son said "Yeah," and went to sit in another part of the room.

Mom was really striking out here. She just sat and watched TV with him for a while, thinking of what to do. Finally she realized that she was a direct speaker and her son was a lot like her. Direct speakers aren't comfortable with the roundabout approach; it can feel vaguely sneaky and unsavory. So she just laid it out for him: "Are kids going over there to drink and party? I need you to be honest with me, because I'm concerned about your well-being. We've always been open, so I'm laying my cards on the table. How about you?"

That worked. He shifted around a little, but he looked her in the eye and said "Yes, they do." She stayed calm and let him talk. It seemed that the parents knew all about it and let kids come there to drink and stay the night, both boys and girls. He wasn't into drinking himself, but he was worried about his friends getting in over their heads.

This was a tough one, because she not only had to talk with him about the problems of teenage drinking, but also had to address his becoming a baby-sitter for his friends. The two of them worked a deal. She wouldn't report the parents and she'd let him go there one more time, but he had to be home by curfew with no drinking.

She had to listen to the real teenage problems of conflicting loyalties and have the courage to trust her son to stick to his part of the bargain. But it took their trust to a new level. It also impressed her husband once he realized what had been going on, and made it possible for them to deal with the issue as a united front.

Extreme Measures

Eliot was the corporate manager who earlier had managed to pull the downsizing meeting out of a tailspin. He was in class when someone else talked about a therapy session in which she'd taken her husband on her lap and asked him to talk to her. I'd never heard of such a thing, but it seemed to work for her.

A few weeks later Eliot, in his corporate suit, came in with the story of his eighteen-year-old son who'd been storming around the house because he'd lost his wallet. Finally Eliot asked his son into his study, closed the door and had his son sit on his lap—this big, 6-foot-plus black teenager.

(Class: "You didn't!")

(Eliot: "I did!")

Then Eliot asked his son why he was so angry.

The son blurted out, "I know, you're Mr. Big Shot, you never do anything wrong, why don't you just light into me and get it over with!" Eliot realized this was what his son was expecting, so he explained he wasn't going to do that. He just wanted to hear why he was so upset.

After a few tries, his son came out with it. Along with his wallet, he'd lost his American Express card. His dad had gotten him the card, he was so proud of it, and now he'd blown it and let the whole family down. His father was going to tell him he was an idiot and he'd never get another credit card again.

Eliot hadn't a clue his son was feeling this way. Losing a wallet could happen to anybody. They talked about what to do: call American Express, call the driver's license office, and see who needed to be notified to get this straightened out. Then his son could handle it like an adult.

I'm still not sure what to make of this technique, but if it got through to a storming eighteen-year-old it might be worth having on file. If you don't want to try taking the kid on your lap, then you might try playing catch or brushing their hair, some reminder of happier days. It may not be for the corporate world, although the thought of this approach at the U.N. Security Council has immense appeal.

Bad History

If there's been bad history, expect to work harder to get your answer.

A production manager was incensed with a sales rep because he kept getting left out of client meetings. He was the guy who was ultimately responsible for delivering the product, so it was crucial that he be included in these meetings. After the third time it happened, he went to confront her.

The production manager insisted on getting advance warning on these meetings. The sales rep was throwing files in her briefcase, not looking up at him and telling him she really didn't have time to talk. She said she went looking for him last time and didn't find him, so she just went ahead with the meeting.

The production manager pointed out that there was another guy with a tight schedule and he always got notified of these meetings. Why couldn't she notify him at the same time? She said she'd try to remember. The production manager nearly flooded; he didn't want her to *try* to notify him, he wanted her to do it!

Realizing this wasn't working, he took a breath and tried a different approach. He needed her to stop fighting him on this one. Not knowing what else to say, he asked if something was going on that he didn't know about.

The sales rep sighed (probably monitoring herself) and put down her briefcase. She seemed to look for a way to get out of it, then just told the truth. The problem was that she'd worked with other production managers and in these meetings they would question everything she said. She'd be talking to the client and the production manager would say, "That's ridiculous!" and make her look stupid. These were important clients and she couldn't have her own people undermining her.

The next step was to listen to the answer. The production manager knew she'd never worked with him, but he could see her point just the same. This was something she couldn't afford. So they talked about how he could bring up questions so that they sounded like questions, and not like he was doubting her. Before this was over she apologized for taking things out on him, and a week before the next meeting he got an e-mail with the proper time and place.

The last step was to have the courage to act on what he heard. The entire deal would fall apart if he didn't do exactly what he said, no slips and no excuses. He was careful to do no inadvertent monitoring and stayed away from indirect gaffs. The meeting went well, and their working relationship changed.

Hard Listening

Then, sometimes, you need to listen to yourself.

A tech worker was going through a miserable downsizing with her company. Her manager had already been let go and the rest of the department was leaderless and drifting, waiting for the ax to fall.

Each day she found it harder to get up in the morning without her manager to notice what time she got in. Soon she was showing up at 10 and sometimes 11 o'clock in the morning.

One day after she'd dragged herself in at 11:30, one of her colleagues stopped in at her office and told her in no uncertain terms that he was tired of covering for her. They were all upset about the lay-offs, but that was no excuse for dumping her work on the rest of them. Then he turned and stalked out.

She was burning with shame and anger. How dare he talk to her that way! She had worked hard to get her position and she wasn't about to be talked to like that! She furiously plotted when she could see him next and the cutting things she would say.

As she fumed she thought about different questions that would make him regret it: Where do you get off? Who do you think you are? But she realized these were all rhetorical questions. She really didn't care about the answer; she just wanted to pound him.

She was searching for a more appropriate question when a small voice inside her posed a new one: "What if he's right?"

This was the last thing she wanted to hear, but she steeled herself and followed where it led. She'd been running late for at least two months, ever since her boss was let go. Other people had had to cover her calls all the time she wasn't there. Evidently no one had reported her; at least she hadn't heard about it.

The more she thought about it, the more she found the questions weren't for him but for herself. Why was she acting like this? She had worked hard for her position—so why was she throwing her responsibility away? Of course she was upset that her boss was fired, especially knowing she would be next. But everyone else was going through it too; she was dumping the burden on the very people who didn't deserve it.

Next she had to have the courage to act on what she heard: she was going to have to pull herself together and stop all this. Worse, she was going to have to go back to this guy and apologize. To her credit, she did it.

Finally, she realized she had to find the courage to get out of there and not just wait for the ax to fall, because she was turning into someone she didn't want to be.

The tech worker wasn't just flooding because she'd been chewed out. Shame had sent her into a tailspin. By asking these questions she inadvertently backed into the truth, which was not a very comfortable thing.

She was in the transition zone, but she pulled out without disgracing herself. She found the decent thing to do, which at that moment took a lot of courage; but it was easier to live with in the long term.

Staying in Problem-Solving

There was a case with divorced parents, who shared custody of a twelve-year-old daughter. The father had custody on alternate weekends and holidays, or on weeks when the mom would travel on business.

Sometimes the father would miss picking up his daughter for their weekends together, and would then want to get her on a weekend scheduled for the mother. Of course, mom would resent it and insist on sticking to schedule. They'd escalate straight into psychological warfare: name-calling, stonewalling, threatening to withhold child support, the works.

This time, before things got carried away, the mother stopped and asked her ex what the problem was. He just said that he had other plans than picking up the girl.

The mother's first impulse was to go ballistic: "And what do you have to do that's more important than picking up your daughter?" But she stopped herself and re-thought her response. She asked if he could think of another alternative.

He paused, then answered obliquely: He didn't think the girl liked coming to see him. She only came over because she had to, and she always talked about how she couldn't wait until she could go back home to her mother.

OK, so that was the issue: he was picking a fight with the mom because he was feeling rejected by his daughter. Now, the mom had to admit he had probably mentioned things like this before, but she hadn't paid attention. She just thought, "She's your daughter. Fend for yourself." But this time she took it differently. She told her ex that actually the girl seemed to like to see her dad, but she'd probably say something like that to get him mad.

Then it dawned on the mother that, back when they were married, she used to say things like that to get him mad and her daughter was a lot like her. The girl looked like her and talked like her, and it must be pretty tough on him to deal with this re-incarnation who walked into his house.

So to bring his focus back to the girl, the mother started telling him about his daughter: her school, her hobbies, what she liked and disliked, things that set her apart as an individual. She'd never done this before—she'd always just thought, "Let him figure it out for himself." But he wasn't good at figuring out his daughter; he was still upset about the divorce.

They finally were able to talk this through without getting into a fight. Between them they decided that their girl was growing up, and maybe they should ask her where she wanted to stay on some of these weekends–maybe even at her grandpa's or grandma's. But they were able to handle it like civilized adults.

Fairness Back at Problem-Solving

As the mom in this case caught herself, she became progressively more fair to her ex, which perhaps hadn't been such a priority in the past. Remember, if someone shifts on one line of the continuum, they're likely to shift on all lines. That's exactly what this mother did. She first became engaged in problem-solving, then stopped withholding information, then started negotiating and focusing on a clean fight.

This same unexpected desire for fairness surfaced with the employee who didn't like to take direction. This employee had never before admitted that he was too rigid or that there was any problem in his own behavior. But now he offered to change, without prompting.

When people move back to problem-solving, an unanticipated sense of justice may appear. The manager hadn't pointed out that the employee was being rigid or refusing to cooperate (actually he had, many times in the past, but by this time he'd given up mentioning it). The employee offered it himself and followed it with a concrete plan.

Now why did he do that? No one asked him to make this concession. Yet this kind of thing keeps coming up as people shift back to problem-solving.

You make a concession, like listening. The other side checks to see if this could possibly be true, that you're not just running a con. Then they make a concession. Why do they do that? Maybe they knew all along they weren't perfect, they just didn't want to say so and get clobbered for it. Maybe they'd been wanting to back off their position for some time, and didn't have any way to do it and save face. Maybe it's tit for tat, and if you're going to do something decent, they will, too. All I know is that it keeps happening with this technique, so don't be surprised if it happens to you.

If someone makes an unexpected concession, *tell them you appreciate it.* Don't brush it aside, don't turn it down, don't say they needn't bother. For some people, making a concession is a revolutionary act. Make them feel that it was a excellent move, not something unimportant. If you treat it as something trivial they may never do it again.

Every Problem Can Be Solved

Janet was in civil service at level 12 and found, checking the books, that her actual work was at a higher rank that paid better. So she went to talk it over with her boss.

Her boss agreed with the bulk of the description, but pointed out that there were two crucial things Janet didn't do: spend time on big-picture issues (which she disliked) and work with a VP whom she hated.

This wasn't what Janet had expected to hear; she could almost physically feel her body fighting it. She felt a little schizophrenic, making herself listen while feeling her body shut the words out. It made it almost impossible to talk, but she got through the meeting and went outside for a walk.

Once she got her flooding under control, she couldn't argue with what her boss had to say, but that was beside the point. *She had wanted her boss to say something else.* She wanted the upgrade, period. She wasn't emotionally prepared for what she got, and she could feel her system shut down when faced with it.

Looking at it calmly, she could see that her boss wasn't opposed to giving her the upgrade, but she was going to have to take on different priorities. Yet she liked things the way they were, especially when it came to avoiding the VP.

On her way back in she saw the VP down the hall, which would normally be her cue to duck into an empty office. But, she told herself, no time like the present. So she went up to him and told him about a project she knew would pique his interest. That put her on his schedule, on her terms, and she began to make inroads from there.

In this case, Janet needed to delegate details (she liked details) and be brave and patient enough to work with someone powerful whom she really disliked. Qualifying for this promotion was going to take real effort on her part, in a way that she hadn't anticipated.

Bevel refers to two basic assumptions: Every problem can be solved, and every problem merits its own solution. A big problem merits a big effort, and a small problem merits a small effort.

He then asks: Who would we need to be to solve that problem? In many cases we might need to be patient, understanding and forgiving—and we don't want to do that. It's more satisfying to be cranky and abrupt, and huffy if we're in the mood. It's fun to get high and mighty and be totally unreasonable. It feels great. But it won't solve the problem.

If it's a minor problem, Bevel says we're off the hook: we don't have to change and we don't have to fix it. It's small and not worth the effort. But if it's a genuinely minor problem, then we also have to stop complaining and worrying about it. If it isn't worth the effort to solve, then it's not worth imposing on other people to ask them to listen to us gripe. If we decline to put in the effort to fix the problem, we give up our right to complain about it.

A common paradox is when people describe a large, important problem, complain about it at great length, and then expend no effort whatsoever to fix it.

If something's large and valuable—like, say, the love of your children—then you may need to do hard, challenging things to get it. You can always try the quick fix and buy the kids' affections, or give them empty compliments to bolster their self-esteem. You can take advice without questioning it, inherit values without testing them, react with rage when provoked and do all the easy, obvious things. You can make terrible mistakes and never admit them, not even to yourself. You can do all these easy things and raise kids you don't even want to know yourself.

There is a writer's rule: bad writing is every bit as much work as good writing. Taking the easy way out is every bit as much work as struggling through the hard stuff. You just pay for it in different ways.

Working Limits

The Principle of Communication works wonderfully well with level one problem-solving or level two power plays, and it fails outright by level three. That doesn't make it a bad technique, just a tactic that's not right for blind behavior.

For example, a businessman had a cousin who may have had a drinking or drug problem; certainly something was very wrong. In any case, he sent her some supplies to help her get back on her feet, and instead of using them as promised, she sold the stuff and kept the money.

The businessman found out about it and sat down with her to give her the chance to come clean. After some small talk he asked, "Are you sure there isn't something you want to tell me?" His cousin smiled and dodged. Then he asked, "Are you *sure* there isn't something you want to tell me?" and the woman dodged again. Finally he leaned forward and said, "ARE YOU SURE there isn't something you want to tell me." Her mouth dropped open. She hedged, stammered, then came out with the whole story.

The businessman gave her The Lecture and made it clear she could pay up and set things right. The cousin was humble, abashed and promised to make restitution.

Your guess is correct: he never saw that money again. The last I heard she wasn't returning phone calls and he was considering court.

For a brief moment it looked as though something may have gotten through, but unfortunately it was only The Lecture, which was all the satisfaction that businessman was going to get for his money. He got hustled; it was nothing more than manipulation and whining, the standard unhealthy skill set.

However, this breakdown wasn't a flaw in the Principle of Communication. Addictions place the conflict at level three, where this technique is bound to fail.

Level three conflict is defined by blind behavior. People can't very well tell you a solution because they don't know what they're doing; they're groping their way through the dark. An addict doesn't know why she keeps using, and may not even see it as a problem. An abuser truly believes it's the victim's fault. There are no hidden insights to be had. They can't tell you the truth because they don't know it themselves.

At level three, people find themselves caught in a vicious circle, tripping over the same problems in the same ways, with very little understanding of what they're doing or why. They can't help you get your bearings; they're walking in circles, lost.

For instance, the right question in the last case might be, "Cousin, why are you acting like this?" And the real answer might be "You know, I've been drinking so much I've gotten myself in an awful fix. I can't seem to stop. Maybe I'd better check myself into rehab."

This answer might be perfectly true, and the businessman's odds of hearing it are something like 10,000 to one. The cousin can't tell him the truth because she can't see it herself.

Bigots do the same kind of circling in the dark, only they sound more ferocious about it. Let's say you interrupt someone mid-tirade and say, "Joe, what is this with you and black people (or Jews/women/foreigners/gay folk)? You start talking and steam comes out of your ears, your eyes roll back in your head. Where do you get all this, anyway?"

Joe doesn't answer, "I dunno. Never thought about it. Suppose my dad did the same thing. I guess that's where I picked it up." You simply don't get this kind of answer. Instead, Joe turns the venom on you.

In order for the Principle of Communication to work the other side needs some small dose of self-awareness, but that's exactly what's missing at level three. They're blind to their own behavior and they can't break out of this self-perpetuating loop. At best, like the businessman, you may get what appears to be a momentary breakthrough, but it won't mean much. Like him, you'll soon find yourself right back where you started from, with a long, hard struggle ahead of you. That means you're now caught in the vicious circle, too.

Use this tactic for mere power plays; blind behavior requires something more. That will be covered in the rest of the book.

What to Remember

Bevel's Principle of Communication is a deceptively simple three-part technique.

1) Ask the right question.
2) Listen to the answer.
3) Have the courage to act on what you hear.

- **Refusing to listen** or change is a sign of weakness, not strength. Listening and changing demands courage, strength and moral caliber. Stonewalling can be done by any idiot.

- **Think before agreeing.** Automaticly agreeing is also not a sign of courage. Courage may mean checking the statement or thinking it over and coming back with a counteroffer.

- **Avoid monologues.** Dialogues create the breakthroughs.

- **Yes or no questions** won't work. Ask open-ended questions.

- **Rhetorical questions** don't count.

- **Ask three questions** at the minimum. Don't expect to find the right question on the first try.

- **The atmosphere will change** when you hit the right question. Often the air goes electric.

- **Every problem merits its own solution.** A small problem merits a small effort, and a large problem merits a large effort.

- **Don't expend massive effort** on a minor problem, and don't beg off with platitudes when faced by a major problem. If you honestly believe something isn't worth the effort to fix it, let it go and move on.

What Works Where

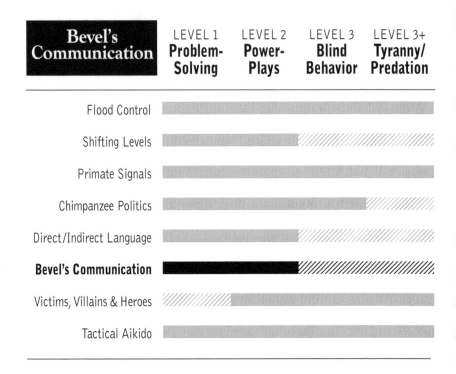

Bevel's Communication	LEVEL 1 Problem-Solving	LEVEL 2 Power-Plays	LEVEL 3 Blind Behavior	LEVEL 3+ Tyranny/ Predation
Flood Control	████	████	████	████
Shifting Levels	████	████	/////	/////
Primate Signals	████	████	████	████
Chimpanzee Politics	████	████	████	/////
Direct/Indirect Language	████	████	/////	/////
Bevel's Communication	████	████	/////	/////
Victims, Villains & Heroes	/////	████	████	████
Tactical Aikido	████	████	████	████

For the Principle of Communication to work, the other side needs some small dose of self-awareness, which is exactly what's missing at level three. This technique works well at levels one or two, but shouldn't be tried outside that range.

Chapter Eight

Blind Behavior and the Vicious Circle

> *"You go back, Jack, do it again*
> *Wheels turning round and round,*
> *You go back, Jack, do it again....."*
> —*Steely Dan*

The vicious circle is the natural result of blind behavior, like walking in circles when lost in the woods. Since people can't see what they're doing, they keeping making the same mistakes over and over again. This leads to an awful feeling of deja vu, as if the past keeps coming back to haunt you, as if dead events and dead people keep coming back to run your life and do it badly.

This is the curse of the geographic solution. You move to the opposite end of the country trying to escape your problems, only to find them sitting in the living room reading the local paper.

Even huge sums of money have little effect on blind behavior, as has been discovered with social service agencies and corporate reform. Studies on lottery winners find that within five years most winners are back where they started.

The vicious circle appears in large conflicts and small. Northern Ireland, the Middle East, addictions, abuse and bigotry all have a strangely circular feel. They're self-reinforcing and self-perpetuating, afflictions that feed on themselves and never quite go away.

A vicious circle is not a one-sided thing; it's not just about cruelty or ignorance or retaliation. By nature it has several different sides, along with an ability to keep itself turning. To understand it we need to look at it from 360 degrees, to see the strange and unexpected things that occur.

Blind Spots and Cultural Norms

The vicious circle can start with lower level conflict and be triggered by nothing more than cultural differences. It's like the tourist at the Mexican market who doesn't speak Spanish, so she keeps talking louder in English. The louder she talks, the less people listen. It's the quicksand effect: the harder she struggles the faster she sinks.

I did a mediation between Romanian landlords and an elderly black church lady who had been their tenant for a number of years. The tenant was on social security, and one month her check was late. She told her landlords about the late check; they waited the five day minimum and served eviction papers. I saw them in court. The church lady was outraged that her landlords should file for eviction, while the Romanians were standing by their rights.

Now, black church goers have a high-trust culture. As an elderly church lady, she had earned trust and was entitled to it. Trust was a mark of her place in the world and a sign of her hard-won respectability.

Romanians have a low-trust culture. Only children trust, and it would be insulting to ask businesspeople to trust. It would be like asking them to be childish or stupid.

You should have seen the discussions between these two. The landlords wanted her as a tenant. The tenant liked the place and had the cash in her purse. The money had to travel three feet across the table in order to complete the deal and it couldn't make the trip.

We would be finalizing the last details and the church lady would say, "Why didn't you just trust me on this?" and the Romanians would burst into sputtering indignation. I would get them calmed down and back on track, and then one of the Romanians would mutter, "Just expected us to trust you, I suppose," and the black church lady would erupt in outrage.

Even I had a place in the vicious circle, because even though I knew exactly what they were doing, I was so worn out from all the explosions I never stopped to explain it to them. By then I was flooding myself, so I didn't think to stop the action and explain what they were doing. Yet without that information the odds were high that the same kind of problem would happen again.

Ricochet

Decent people fall into these traps once blind behavior comes into play. Worse, the quicksand effect comes into play, where the harder people struggle the faster they sink.

Let's say, for example, that I'm the dictator of a small country where the normal price of bread is one dollar. Only this year the harvest failed, so the price of bread jumps to two dollars. Now I'm a benign dictator and I care about my country. I don't like this because my people are going hungry, and privately, I worry that it makes me look bad. This could undermine my regime. So I order the price of bread back to one dollar.

Any economist will tell you that this won't solve the problem. In fact, bread will disappear from the shelves altogether and reappear on the black market at three dollars a loaf.

As dictator, of course, this makes me furious. I just ordered the price of bread down and now people are paying three dollars a loaf. I think these insufferable merchants are out to defy me and provoke me beyond endurance.

Showing I mean business, I order soldiers into the shops to strong-arm the merchants. And what happens? Some bread reappears on the shelves at one dollar, but the rest goes deeper underground where the price of bread spikes to four dollars a loaf.

The harder I try to force down the price of bread, the faster it rises in real terms. If I completely lose my head and hammer down at all costs I can force the issue, but I will also cripple the economy. This is what Stalin managed to do in the Soviet Union.

The problem is that I've missed something. Although I'm a dictator, I'm not alone in this decision. The invisible hand of the market is at work. The harder I push down, the harder the invisible hand will push up and my best efforts will lead to the opposite of what I want. My hard work backfires.

Now consider this case with a small difference. Let's say I'm not a dictator and don't have the power to order price controls; instead I have to go to the legislature for approval. The legislature turns me down cold and says: "Snap out of it. Open your eyes! The harvest has failed. If you want to lower the price of bread, import some more grain."

Now, if I had absolute power I would dissolve the legislature for talking to me this way, and do even more harm to the country. But I don't have that power so I'm forced to consider their opinion. I don't like it but I'm forced to settle down, and this turns out to be good for me. Chastened, I stand down the army and bring in grain. The invisible hand is now working with me and the price of bread goes down.

As dictator I believed I need more power. In fact, I needed less power and a feedback loop. With absolute power I resort to force, but with less power I must listen to other perspectives and use common sense. In short, less force, used wisely, delivers better results.

Each form of conflict operates in different ways, and level three is counterintuitive. It looks as if it's sensible to use force, but that will get me the opposite of what I want. With quicksand, the natural reaction is to jerk your foot away, but that will only pull you in deeper. The wise advice is counterintuitive: calm down. Don't thrash. Conserve your energy until you reach something solid. Use force only as a last resort, because you may not like the reaction you get.

At level three there's a wicked ricochet. We see versions of this everyday and attribute it to people trying to drive us insane.

Your teenaged daughter takes up with some awful boy, so you forbid her to ever see him again. What happens? She sneaks out to find him that very night. If you hammer down and make things worse, you can convince her to run away and marry him.

Palestinians attack Israelis in order to get their land back, and so Israelis build a wall that takes another 10% of the West Bank. Israelis want peace from the Palestinians and so send soldiers into Palestinian villages, so Palestinians blow up Israeli markets.

This isn't perverse human nature. This is the norm at level three: there's a wicked ricochet. You think your problem is this opponent who is trying to drive you mad, but the bigger problem is actually the quicksand sucking at both of your feet.

Anyone from the outside could tell the Israelis and Palestinians that quicksand is about to pull them under. But they're both thrashing, furious that things aren't getting better.

The solution is counterintuitive: Settle down. Move away from the quicksand, don't go in deeper. Throw a line to the people thrashing, but don't go in yourself. Hunt out the skills at level one, because you'll need something solid to hold onto.

Problem-solving is an antidote to blind behavior. Consider my traits as dictator. I think of myself a benevolent leader, but power has undermined my judgment. I'm more upset about looking ineffectual than I am about the true state of the country, which is lacking grain. I'm probably flooding as I give my orders, and consequently options disappear. I become rigid as I send more troops, and resort to accusation and overkill and rather than negotiation with the merchants, who would tell me straight away that they need more grain. I do not ask how to work things out, I strive to prove I'm Right, even as I'm demonstrate mightily that I'm wrong.

And yet for all this I honestly mean well. I genuinely love my country. But there's no counterbalance for my dictatorial powers, and having lost my head there's no one to stop me from wrecking things. Blind to my own behavior, I can't see what I'm doing. I think I'm being a hero, but I've forgotten to check to see if that's true. And the more I act out the more I frighten people and the less willing they'll be to tell me the truth.

Level three is not just about evil people, although some frightening types appear in this range. It's really about not being able to see what you're doing.

Reality and the Vicious Circle

Across the range of blind behavior one finds an increasingly flawed view of reality. Arthur Anderson executives, after being forced out of business over Enron, sincerely felt they were scapegoats; yet this was not the first time they'd been caught and the company was already on probation for other problems at a different firm. Cardinal Law, caught shuffling pederasts from point to point, seemed aggrieved that the press wasn't more understanding of the difficult position he was in.

This stalwart refusal to face reality can leave one suspended between amazement and despair. It helps to know how the brain operates.

Most of us assume our brains are like cameras, recording the world. Brain researchers now understand that's not the case. In fact, at least two different parts of the brain work together to give us our grip on reality. One part is in the logical left side of the brain, which reinforces what we already believe: I know my side is correct and everything's OK. Therefore, all facts prove that my side is correct and everything's OK.

Hopefully this is balanced by a section in the opposite side of the brain that registers exceptions when things are not fine; when in fact, when something is terribly wrong. In street terms, this side has the shit-detector. This side can smell a rat.

With blind behavior, this system goes haywire.

Dr. Vilayanur Ramachandran is a neuroscientist who has done fascinating work with patients who develop a condition called anosognosia, which follows a certain kind of stroke. Someone who had previously led a normal life would abruptly acquire denial typical of an addict or cult member. For instance, Supreme Court Justice William O. Douglas was in the hospital with a stroke when he told a visitor he'd just kicked a 40-yard field goal. Half his body was paralyzed.

With anosognosia, the brain is unable to notice there's a problem. In one experiment, partly paralyzed stroke patients were asked to do a two-handed task, like tying a bow. Someone without the condition would refuse: How absurd! How could they tie a bow with one hand paralyzed? Yet those with anosognosia would try over and over, never noticing that only one hand was moving. When they finally gave up they'd brush off the matter, saying they didn't feel like tying bows or their arthritis was acting up.

Another interesting point was that when faced with an inescapable fact, patients often found someone else to blame. For instance, their left arms might be paralyzed and lying inert in their laps, so they'd demand to know whose arm it was. They'd insist the arm belonged to their brother or the doctor and order it be taken away. One man was startled to find himself on the floor after he threw his own leg out of bed.

Two different factors seem to be at work. First, the step-by-step logic was still running gerbil-like, proving everything was fine. Second, the alarm mechanism was disconnected, so the brain couldn't tell it had stopped making sense.

Conversations with these patients have an eerie feel, like logic from a different dimension. A doctor in Italy reported a case where a stroke patient insisted his paralyzed arm belonged to the doctor. The doctor finally picked up the limp hand and held it up between his own two hands. He asked the patient if he'd ever seen a man with three hands. The patient replied, "A hand is the extremity of an arm. Since you have three arms, it follows that you must have three hands."

Perhaps it's pure coincidence, but the same eerie logic appears at level three. The pattern is most striking not in perpetrators but in victims.

One woman lost an arm and a leg after her boyfriend tried to kill her with his van. Her daughter witnessed this and the man himself didn't deny it. The woman petitioned to get her boyfriend out of jail because it was interfering in their relationship.

A mother who loved her daughter very much was shocked to hear her husband had sexually abused the girl. Yet once she heard her daughter screaming and walked into her husband's bedroom, to find him standing over her partly undressed. The husband explained they were just playing a game, so the wife left them alone and shut the door.

These people were not brain dead. Their alarms had been turned off.

Colliding with Reality

People engaged in blind behavior believe their own lies. There's no talking them out of it, that gerbil-logic is invulnerable. Contrary to what you might think, such a person does not need your advice. They won't hear a thing you say, anyway. What they need is to get their brains working again. Often the best way to do that is to let them slam into reality.

One addictions counselor had great success with alcoholics sent over from court, who are usually difficult cases. He'd talk to them about going into treatment, and of course they'd deny having a drinking problem. The counselor would nod and start filling out the paperwork sending them back to court. The alcoholics would say, "Hey, you can't do that. They'll send me to jail."

The counselor would explain patiently that he'd been operating under a misunderstanding. He believed they had a disease called alcoholism and needed treatment. Instead, they pointed out that nothing of the sort was going on. Since they weren't acting that way because of a disease, they clearly were acting that way because they were criminals. So they shouldn't be in a treatment program at all, they should be in jail; and he went back to filling out the forms.

They went into treatment.

Sonia Johnson tells a story about a woman had been battered so many times she'd become a regular at the emergency room. The staff had come to like her, but no one could talk her into leaving her husband. She always went back, and she always ended up again in the emergency room. It was quite literally a vicious circle.

Finally, someone sat down and talked to her about who would be the best person to bring up her children. Obviously one of these beatings would kill her and her husband would go to jail, so someone would have to look after the kids. Who did she think would be best to do that?

She finally left her husband.

In this approach, there's no accusation and the voice is very calm, but nothing is done to buffer the blow. Let this person collide with reality and see if they can't figure things out.

A similar approach is used in hostage negotiation, which is clearly a form of tyranny. The hostage negotiator stays calm and reasonable, and never says "No" but also never says "Yes." He certainly never argues. At some point the gunman looks around and realizes he's alone with no back-up, there's no way out and there are guys dressed like trees standing outside his window. At that point the quality of the negotiation changes. The gunman stops demanding fresh ammunition and starts trying to find a safe way to surrender.

You'd Never Know They Could Negotiate

At level three there's a low but still existing ability to negotiate; you'd just never know it from the way they behave. One way to get past that is to block all accusation and manipulation and set the boundaries so they have to negotiate.

One woman had a teenage step-son who was doing drugs, getting in trouble with the law and generally acting out of control. The first wife had custody, but the boy would visit on weekends when he'd provoke regular screaming fights with the step-mom.

The boy's mother didn't know what to do with him and a lot of things weren't getting done. For instance, he was 18 and still didn't know how to drive. His mother wouldn't teach him, since he'd only get drunk and drive up a tree. But still it was humiliating for an 18-year-old to have to wait for his mother to give him a lift.

The boy wanted to leave his mom and move in at the step-mom's house; she, of course, was beside herself. If she said yes, her life would be in shambles, but if she said no, her husband would be furious and she'd be the evil step-mother. She felt trapped either way.

The first thing I asked her to do was to consider herself a negotiator and create a winning position for herself. What would it take for her to enjoy having this kid in the house? This was an alien concept, but eventually she could construct a picture. Basically, she needed the kid to behave like a responsible human being. That meant no drugs in the house and no trouble with the police. He would need to pull his own weight, do his own laundry and clean his own room. She was OK with teaching him to drive, but for his part, he would need to get a job so he could buy his own gas and cover part of the insurance.

These were reasonable expectations for an 18-year-old, and she worked on the list with her husband, which put them both on the same team. Her husband actually liked this. He was used to his son and his new wife just screaming at each other, so he saw this as a major step forward.

Next the step-mom and her husband approached the boy with their list. He completely blew them off. He was watching TV and wouldn't even look up, just kept changing the channel.

The step-mom knew she was being provoked, so she didn't react. She and her husband let him know they were willing to talk whenever he was ready, but that he wasn't moving in until they'd worked out the ground rules. Then they went about their business.

A few weeks later the kid asked again about moving in, and they explained that they still needed to work out the rules. The kid was visibly uncomfortable, but this time he sat down and went over the list with them. He didn't seem to know what to say or do. He knew how to curse and defy them, but he didn't seem to know how to talk things through or handle give and take.

With nothing really settled, he went back to his mom's house. A few days later the step-mom got the news: He wasn't moving in. The boy had joined the marines. (This was peacetime.)

The woman again was beside herself—now this kid had walked out of negotiations. Actually, he'd come up with a perfectly legitimate move. In negotiation terms it's called BATNA: the Best Alternative to Negotiated Agreement. He had looked at the situation and he'd looked at his alternatives, and he decided to take an alternative.

The step-mom hadn't expected this, but it was a perfectly good life choice. In the marines he would learn about personal responsibility and picking up after himself, and he'd have to think twice about drugs or picking fights with strangers. His parents wouldn't be writing the rules, the marines would. Perhaps at 18 he didn't know how to straighten himself out and needed some help to do that.

Taking charge of his life seemed to stabilize the kid. He stopped fighting with his step-mom and started talking with his father to figure out how to handle his prospective paycheck. They worked out a plan for how much he could spend and how much he could save, so that when he got out of the service he could buy his own house.

For her part, the step-mom stopped getting pulled into endless fights and insisted on give-and-take. Most of all, she stopped focusing on all the things the kid did wrong, which she couldn't control, and started watching her own behavior, which she could control. That brought her to solid ground where she could make things change.

Creating Limits

Limits disappear at level three. The step-mother with the out-of-control stepson had been talking fruitlessly for years, but she had never set effective limits. She got his attention once he understood he would not move until he was ready to follow normal rules.

In a similar way it does very little good to talk or reason with someone who goes into rage seizures at the mention of race or religion. What's needed is a concrete limit—action rather than words. Say, "Uncle Harry, I love you and I really like to hear your stories, but when you start talking about race (religion, your ex-wife) things really get out of hand. So I love you, but if you get started again I'm going to have to leave the room. And we can check in sometime later."

Then when Uncle Harry loses it again (he will), don't fight with him. Say, "Sorry, I can't do this," and leave.

It does no good to argue with Uncle Harry. He's flooding and can't hear you. Speak with your feet: Leave.

Setting limits at level three can affect what seems to be an impossibly out of control situation. One man described his alcoholic father who had an insane temper. He got crazy when he drank, gibbering mad with a fondness for butcher knives. This son didn't go to Stephen King movies when he grew up because he still had those movies playing in his head.

But once when the son was small, his father backed someone into a corner and his older brothers called the police who took the father to jail. He got out again, but he spent the night in the lock-up which he didn't like at all. Later he even talked about how much he didn't like it.

Now, he still got drunk and he still had an insane temper, but he never again went so far out of control that they had to call the police. He'd swing at the kids and miss, or he'd grab for knives but he never again tried to corner anyone.

The son was an adult before he realized that his father's behavior changed from the night he spent in the lock-up. Granted he was drunk, but how was it possible that he always missed? Always? He may have looked out of control, but in fact there was some part of him that could hold the line if only to keep himself out of jail. He might have looked insane but he wasn't so crazy that he was going to do something to inconvenience himself.

The classic solution to domestic violence is to call the police the first time it happens. In this range boundaries collapse: set the limit.

The Feedback Loop

Previously, there were no checks and balances on this crazy drunk. There was no adult to say, "All right, put the knife down or you're going into a straightjacket," no recovery program to take him in hand. There were only his inner restraints and they clearly weren't functioning very well.

Checks and balances are missing in this range. Checks and balances operate as a feedback loop, but in blind behavior the feedback loop is damaged. Normal feedback enables us all to check our bearings and stay on course. Without normal feedback, it's all too easy to lose one's moral compass.

Consider the surgeon who casually humiliates his patients; no one informs him that this kind of behavior is unacceptable. The toxic CEO does not have a staff who can tell him he's gone too far, or an independent board to let him know he's flirting with disaster. The film star who walks out on restaurant checks doesn't have the manager stopping her at the door. The addict does not have the enabler cut off the cash flow, any more than the abuser has his victim drop him in his tracks.

Not that there isn't feedback going on. People have tried talking to the surgeon, the CEO, the film star, addict and abuser. But at level three, conversations don't work very well. If people can't see their own behavior, they also can't follow your line of reasoning.

It's said that addictions laugh at boundaries, but in these cases words don't create the limits. Actions do.

Not the Right Action

You'll notice that I keep stressing calm, when the natural reaction in this range is fury, despair or indignation. Emotions are important and have to be dealt with in some appropriate way, but lashing out is seldom going to get you what you need especially in this range. There's simply too much ricochet. And anger, driven by entitlement, will make things much, much worse.

Entitlement may start as a reflex reaction. Someone's mean to you and so you're mean right back; you're entitled to be mean. And since you're entitled, to make a point you're a lot a more mean to the other person, or someone who looks just like them. That way they'll remember you. And they do. They're twice as mean the next time around.

This is what plays in Northern Ireland, an ugly divorce, or that wretched department down the hall.

The crucial thing is the loop between violation and entitlement. Once I have been wronged I am entitled to get my own back; I no longer have to question if my behavior is fair or right or even reasonable. I *am* right. By reason of my being wronged I am right and everything I do is right, even if it lands me in jail. Then I am more wronged, and still right, and the moment I get out I can go smash something because I've been wronged, and I'm entitled to be right even if I have to kill someone else and maybe myself to prove it.

Remember that cycle between violation and vulnerability? It just got much worse. Two things have happened here. I've started flipping back and forth between being wronged—the violation—and doing wrong—the entitlement. These are opposite ends of a pole with a lot of gray space in between, but I'm not spending time in the gray zone at all. I won't deign to glance at it, even when I can see that I'm driving a situation towards disaster. I can't stop being Right, so I can't back down or look for another solution. Being Right is my due and therefore any mistakes I make are forgivable, because I am fundamentally Right.

Naturally I wouldn't extend that forgiveness to anyone else, because they're wrong, wrong, wrong. They don't count. Only I do. That remarkable egocentricity is back in play.

The central flaw is that I don't pause to examine my own behavior. I don't have to question if what I do is right. I am right, I no longer have to qualify for it. I can do things that are destructive, despicable, shabby beyond words, things that harm people I don't dislike and have perhaps never met, but because I'm right all that's OK. If I want to get even with my brother-in-law and make family holidays miserable to do it, then that's just too bad. I don't have to question who I'm hurting or why I'm indulging myself this way. I'm busy, and being Right, I don't have to trouble with trivial things.

This tunnel vision is typical of level three behavior. We become nearly as blind to our own behavior as if someone in Iceland were doing it. You think *I* ruined Thanksgiving? Well, let me tell you, it wasn't me who ruined Thanksgiving, it was Jack that lousy S.O.B.....

My behavior seems to be controlled by Jack, destiny or possibly aliens from Mars.

Active alcoholics talk about drinking this way. Addicted gamblers talk about gambling this way. And when we've acted out so badly that there isn't an imaginable excuse, then all we can say is that we were Right or that someone else was even worse.

The Conflict Seeds Itself

Once the momentum gets established a strange new characteristic appears: the conflict re-creates itself. The vicious circle is, in fact, a perpetual motion machine.

We tend to look at conflict as an episode, an incident, a single event. But level three doesn't do single incident; it's a chain of events, rooted in the past and stretching into the future. We've been looking at these terrible conflicts as if they were snap shots from a film, and they're not: they're the whole movie. Worse, it's a movie that replays itself.

Blind behavior seeds itself and can travel through generations.

The alcoholic is the son of an alcoholic, who was the son of an alcoholic. Without intervention his children face overwhelming odds of becoming addicted in turn, or of marrying someone with an active addiction.

The child of a wife abuser is likely to be a wife abuser, or is likely to be an abused wife. And their children are apt be as they were, and their children after that. It makes therapy look like a very good investment.

In a similar way national hatreds seed themselves, breeding conflict as culture. The wrongs started in the past become the life and wars of today. The people wronged may be dust and gone, no longer hurting, but the hatred lives on, seemingly lasting forever.

This is a different kind of fight: conflict that lasts beyond the lives of the humans who play it out. The humans become interchangeable, while the conflict becomes the norm. It seems to be an invincible thing, an evil that will not die.

But if we put aside that valid fear, the idea of conflict as a chain gives us a double target. We now have two opportunities to intervene. We can move on the incident itself—the crime or the battle of the moment—or break the link to the future, to the future terrorist, the future child molester, the future addict who will come just as surely as the sun rises in the east. If we can't affect one we can move on the other. This is good, because with something this bad we need all the chances we can get.

Conflict as a Mobius Loop

Blind behavior operates like a Mobius loop, which is a shape that seems to do the impossible. You can make one yourself. It's a strip of paper taped in a loop, with a twist before it's brought together. If you

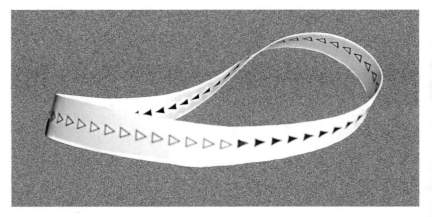

drew a straight line from the start of the loop, you would come back to the beginning on the opposite side from where you started.

With blind behavior, people start out traveling in one direction and effortlessly change into the opposite without ever seeming to change at all.

The following story was related by Daniel Gordis, an American rabbi who moved to Jerusalem. He was standing on a corner, waiting for the light to change, when a car full of young Palestinian women pulled up at the light. Then a car full of young Israeli soldiers, both men and women, stopped next to them. Something had rolled under the seat in the Israeli car, so the young soldiers piled out of the car, laughing, trying to get what was under the seat.

The Palestinian women froze, terrified, as the soldiers scrambled around them, laughing. The rabbi was appalled at the fear he saw on their faces.

In a different decade, it could have been German soldiers laughing at a stoplight, and Jewish women frozen in fear. Or earlier yet, Cossacks laughing and playing with Jews gone sheet white.

It's history as a Mobius loop, doing the impossible, effortlessly changing into the opposite without ever intending to change at all.

Level three conflict clones and turns. This happens with warfare, domestic violence, addictions, sexual abuse, whatever. The victim becomes the abuser becomes the victim, never intending to, never knowing how, ricocheting down a hall of mirrors.

The Fear Trance

The rabbi told a painful story; he clearly cared deeply for Israel and believed in a Jewish nation. But he saw his people caught in a morass, finding no place to turn, no way to stop and no way out. He was describing the quicksand effect, where whatever they did seemed to pull them in deeper. Aside from love in his stories, the other recurring emotion was despair.

One way to track that never-ending loop is to watch how fear controls people.

The following took place in an Alzheimer's agency and amounted to a two minute educational video on race relations in America.

I had a relative with Alzheimer's, so I sat in a tiny reception room with a small couch. A receptionist stood behind the counter. She happened to look a lot like me: my coloration, height, weight and age. We might not look like sisters, but no one would be surprised if we were neighbors or distantly related. We weren't.

A young black woman came in with her mother. Both were tall and well dressed, with beautiful leather coats and the precise good manners of the black middle class. The daughter gave her name to the receptionist and stepped forward to shake hands: that hand hung in space as the receptionist walked off without even looking up at her. It wasn't even that the receptionist snubbed the handshake—she blocked out that young woman so thoroughly she didn't even see the hand.

That hurt from where I sat. If you're in a family with Alzheimer's, you already have all the trouble you need. But the daughter came around the desk to look at some pamphlets and I stood up to offer her mother the couch.

The mother didn't want to sit down, and she may not have understood what I suggested, but she started talking to me rapidly and incoherently. I couldn't follow a word she said. Not knowing what to say, I told she was wearing a beautiful jacket. She broke into an enormous smile and threw her arms wide and hugged me. (She was clearly a lovely woman before she lost her mind.) Then the man I was to meet walked in, and I left.

You have to follow this from different perspectives to get the full craziness of it. The receptionist was so blind that she didn't see the daughter's hand when it was ten inches under her nose. If the daughter had, for a moment, forgotten her manners and slugged her, the receptionist probably would have felt wronged, if not persecuted. Had

I dusted her off and explained that she really had it coming, she would have believed she was surrounded by lunatics.

Now consider the perspective of the young black woman. She walks into an office and gets snubbed without warning. Then another woman, who looks a lot like the first, stands up and offers her mother a seat. The next thing she knows her mother—who is not in her right mind—has thrown her arms around this stranger.

Standing up to give her mother a seat is not a common gesture. Was it because I didn't want to share the couch with her mother? Wasn't that a paranoid assumption? And it would be, only someone who looked just like me had just grossly insulted her not a moment before. So if she does what any normal person does, and bases her next assumption on her last experience, she will come up with a conclusion that's downright crazy. Only what could be more crazy than to be insulted by a perfect stranger just for walking in the door?

How do you keep your equilibrium in that? What is safe? What is real? The whole thing happened in the space of two minutes, and if she were feeling anything at all the daughter would have ended up with emotional whiplash.

Some people handle the emotional whiplash by expecting the worst from everyone, at all times. They are just a teeny bit hostile, but that way at least they don't have to worry that they're crazy, because if you're always hostile you will find the world is hostile back, and that, at least, is predictable. It may not be nice but it's predictable, and you don't have to worry about your mind turning inside-out.

You might say that all the daughter would have had to do was look closely and she would have been able to tell the difference between the receptionist and myself. But it isn't given to us to look into each other's hearts. We only have the surface to work with.

Being human, and flawed, we can only take in a slice of what we see before us. The question is, which slice? The receptionist took in a slice of skin color and felt uncomfortable and defensive. I took in a different slice, that this was a family with Alzheimer's, and felt alert and protective.

We humans are wonderfully egocentric in this. The receptionist could see skin—unlike hers—therefore scary. I could see family-with-Alzheimer's: like me, therefore good.

What makes the process trouble or not depends upon which slice you take. If you take the slice by race or ethnicity, you'll almost always end up with problems.

The receptionist did not mean to be insulting. That's the poison of blind behavior; insult doesn't take effort, it's as natural as breathing. But there was something more. The daughter's hand was directly under her nose, yet she literally didn't see it.

Barbara Fleming, a counselor, describes it as going into a fear trance. The receptionist probably didn't see that hand at all. She wasn't physically afraid of this family. It was the age-old terror of saying something wrong, doing the wrong thing, being offended or offensive, and of course it resulted in her being profoundly offensive herself. Fear blots out reality, even when reality is a tangible fact directly under your nose.

As has been said in other places, fear is a good servant and a poor master, and race is one fear that has mastered us all. Each side will insist that the fear is deserved, that blacks are impossibly hostile, that whites will never give up their privilege, and each side believes the other's argument is patently absurd. Level three conflict loops and turns. And as long as that fear controls us, we are in our blind spots, careening down the highway and crashing into others, oblivious to the damage we've done.

This isn't just limited to race, by any means. This is how women describe men, how men describe women and how other countries describe the USA. Once we get into our blind spots it's a wonder how much damage we can do.

One way out of blind behavior is to dismiss how people look or what they say. Go by what they do.

A pregnant woman wrote to the newspaper, complaining that so-called gentlemen never offered her a seat on the train. Instead she got the offers from kids who looked like gang-bangers and dusty construction workers. She got that exactly wrong. The rough-looking guys were the gentlemen, and the well-dressed guys were the clods.

Blind Spots

We all have our blind spots. Level three conflict happens to everyone, not just wicked people or losers. Every car has a blind spot and every human does, too.

Blind spots are often the points closest to home, where we have our deepest loyalties and passions. The people we love, as well as the people we fear or hate, are where we go blind. Cheating spouses know this very well; people who have gone through bitter divorces get to know it, too.

One way to catch blind spots is to follow the AA rule of three: If three people tell you that you have a drinking problem, it's time to stop and check. If three people tell you your favorite son is pulling cash from the family business, it's time to check the books.

There's no point in asking you to get rid of all your blind spots, since that would ask you to become fully rational around everything you love or hate. That's absurd; you're not a machine. The point is to understand blind spots, not to eradicate them.

Of course it's possible to live effectively despite our blind spots. It's like driving. You stay aware of the blind spot and double-check before you change lanes. It's no more than you'd ask of any other driver.

Remember Bevel's saying: No progress can be made as long as we defer responsibility. That is not to say we can't help someone else; that is to say we can't move forward in our own lives until we come to terms with our own behavior. And first we have to notice what it is.

Survival Skills

It is easy to assume that the crucial problems are on the side of the powerful: blind aggression, blind arrogance or blind complacency. But in fact, the same blindness appears on the victim side: blind co-operation, blind passivity or blind vengeance. It seems obvious that the aggressor must be the one to change: Right and Wrong seems very clear. Right is the victim, Wrong is the abuser. It's us and them, and they need to change, not us.

That's not it. At level three, everyone's trapped in the same quick-sand: abuser and victim, tyrant and slave, active addict and co-dependent. Victims don't get any breaks. Quicksand doesn't care if you're right. It doesn't matter that someone else should change first, that you deserve a break for moral superiority. Perhaps you'll get treated better in the next life, but that's not where you are now.

The solution for good guys at level three is exactly the same as for bad guys: you must become aware of your own behavior. You must stop looking at other people and watch where you become trapped in destructive patterns. The focus is not on them, it's still on you. Your own behavior can get you out of this. No one can do it for you.

Many of the earlier skills we've covered can help accomplish this. For instance, when I was lost in pain and fury with my broken collarbone, I could remember one line only: "I want to work this out." Everything else was lost in a fog. But by hanging on to that single piece, I managed to regain my sanity without humiliating myself in public.

Flood control is another lifeline. Once you stop and check anything about yourself—your heart rate, the quality of your thinking, anything—you have a point of light in the dark. You can use that to get your bearings.

Even chimpanzee behavior can give you that life-saving scrap of self-awareness. You find yourself in an awful spot, pelting head-long for disaster, but you catch yourself at it: you unclench your fists, lean back in your chair. You look at the other person as a raging baboon, and suddenly you needn't be impressed any more. You needn't get hooked in. You don't need to blindly attack or defend, you can find your own way out.

The civil rights workers who overthrew Jim Crow in the South had a concrete grasp of this. They held that no one could be oppressed without their consent, even though that consent may be unknowing; but that the victim's cooperation was essential to oppression. And by withholding cooperation the victim took back power.

Working from Gandhi's principles, they would identify exactly where the cooperation took place. Diane Nash, the non-violent strategist, broke down what was required to have segregated buses. It required black people to get on the bus, pay their money, then take themselves to the back of the bus. Their power and their ability to create change dated from the point they halted their part of the pattern.

As Nash pointed out:

"When Montgomery blacks decided that there weren't going to be segregated buses anymore, there were segregated buses no more. It didn't take any change on the part of the whites when the blacks decided that there would no longer be segregated buses."

This meant whites could sit in a half-empty bus, but they couldn't sit in a segregated bus; and the city of Montgomery couldn't afford half-empty buses. Whites were finally boxed into negotiating, though they swore they never would.

These tactics not only overturned Jim Crow, they touched off the anti-war movement and a series of liberation movements which has altered the nature of life in this country. Those were profoundly effective tactics.

There are ways to free ourselves from the vicious circle. It's not easy; dealing with life at level three means facing terrible things. It's the worst kind of nightmare is to see ourselves becoming our own mothers or fathers, when those were people we'd sworn we'd live down, or finding ourselves becoming the victims that we swore we'd never be. But that's the route to change, and ultimately the hard road to hope.

The next two chapters spell out how to make change happen, how break the vicious circle and spring the traps of level three.

What to Remember

- **The vicious circle** is the natural result of blind behavior. If people can't see what they're doing, they make the same mistakes over and over: Someone flees a miserable marriage, only to marry someone just like their ex. Someone leaves a job they hate, to find a new job they hate just as much. It's the new boss, same as the old boss.

- **In blind behavior,** the feedback loop is damaged. You'll need to re-build a feedback loop. Action will work much better than words.

- **Be careful** about using force in this range. There's a wicked ricochet.

- **At level three** the conflict isn't a single incident but a chain of incidents. It's not just a still shot, it's the whole movie.

- **Level three conflict can seed itself** in the next generation. This creates chronic, endemic problems, but also offers two avenues for solutions: first, address the incident itself, or second, intervene before it's passed to the next carrier.

- **Blind behavior** operates like a Mobius loop. People do what seems to be impossible and end up becoming the people they fear most.

- **Breaking the vicious circle** is too important to be left to the perpetrators. Of course other people ought to change, but we will need to change first. As Bevel says, No progress can be made as long as we defer responsibility.

Chapter Nine

Victims, Villains and Heroes

Consider the most difficult conflicts in the world: abuse, corruption, racism, sexism or religious hatreds. These are entrenched, insolvable struggles, destiny as a Mobius loop, a world of villains, victims and heroes.

And that's exactly the problem.

Take the U.S. in Sudan. We walked in as heroes, turned into villains then ended up victims, all without ever quite knowing what happened. And everyone who joined us got pulled in, too.

This is known as the Toxic Triangle, which was first mapped out by the gifted psychologist Virginia Satir. There are three roles, victim, villain and hero, but they never stay still. The hero becomes villain becomes victim in a dazzling spin of role reversals. Nothing stays put. All roles change in a kind of manic folk dance while the conflict itself spins out of control.

The same pattern plays out in the classic pattern of domestic violence. The husband beats the wife (villain and victim). A neighbor calls the police (enter the hero). The police wrestle down the husband, whereupon he becomes the victim and the police become the villains.

Now the wife becomes the villain for turning in her husband (now the victim), so she turns on the police, which makes her a hero and the police villains. Her husband (still a victim) pleads for her to save him. She recants and refuses to press charges, playing the martyred hero. The police—now victims—walk away in disgust. Neither the husband/victim nor the wife/hero will speak the neighbor, who is now a villain. Perhaps the husband will threaten the neighbor, making the husband the villain once more and the neighbor the victim.

This lasts until the husband beats the wife again, which he will surely do. Shake once and spin.

It's the quicksand effect in action, and the more people struggle the faster they'll sink. The harder they strive as hero or victim, the worse things get. The pattern clones itself, and is perfectly capable of out-living the players as the next generation joins in the dance.

Toxic Triangle

VICTIM

you are here ★

HERO

★ *for the moment*

VILLAIN

Virginia Satir found the key to the chaos: once the triangle starts, there's no stopping it. There are no brakes on this thing. You may start as a hero, but you'll inevitably turn into a villain or victim. Within this system there's no way to win. The solution is to step off the triangle.

In the case of family abuse, police are now specifically trained not to be heroes but simple professionals. They read the husband his rights, take him away whether or not his wife has just switched stories, book the charges and process the paperwork. Professionalism means resisting drama, noting the facts and being careful not to be pulled in any direction. They now walk in knowing that it's quicksand with an undertow, and have specific instructions to keep them from get bogged down.

Moving off the Triangle

There was a married man we'll call Bill, who worked with a woman we'll call Liza. Bill and Liza had an affair, which soon hit trouble. Liza poured out her problems to her best friend who worked at the same office, whom we'll call Samatha. Samantha, wishing to do right by her friend, tried to reconcile Bill and ended up in bed with him herself.

The whole thing exploded at the office Christmas party, attended by Bill, Liza, Samantha and Mrs. Bill, while the rest of the office watched in slack-jawed astonishment.

The resulting uproar did not stop there, but split the office into warring factions. Liza's faction thought Samantha and Bill were villains and Liza was a victim. Samantha's faction thought Liza was a villain and Samantha was a victim. There was a religious set who thought they were all going to hell, and there was another contingent who just wanted to do their work. They were a distinct minority. Bill, of course, was a villain, victim or hero depending on whom he was in bed with at the moment.

The problem was that the office had a deadline with a big bonus if they met it and penalties if they didn't. That bonus made a large percent of their yearly salary, but they weren't going to make that deadline because the place was up for grabs and no one was doing any work.

The manager realized something had to be done, so she called everyone together in a kind of town-meeting. She sat everyone around a conference table and gave each person exactly four minutes to speak his or her mind. The best line came from one of the worker bees: "I'm trying to buy a house right now, and I need this bonus for the down payment. I'm looking at a situation where I may not be able to buy a house for my family because Bill here can't keep it in his pants."

The manager acted as time-keeper, cutting people off mid-rant when their time was up. Once the clock ran out she called an end to the venting and put the question before them: How were they going to get past this? Then she folded her arms and waited.

There was a lot of uneasy shifting, but they finally agreed there was really nothing left to do but get back to work. Liza and Samantha weren't ready to stop fighting, but Bill had had enough and so had everyone else. Bill locked himself in his office and only appeared to hand papers in and out. The drama was broken and the buzz got put on hold. They made the deadline.

The manager could have played hero and banged heads together, but she saw that would only add to the uproar. Instead, she assigned herself a boring, practical role. She let everyone have a say, held the stopwatch, then asked for the plan. The manager stepped off the triangle and insisted that everyone else go with her.

Liza and Samantha were unwilling to stop, but without Bill or the rest of the office they couldn't keep the pot boiling. Rather than letting those two work the crowd, the manager isolated both of them and took them off center stage. The fight was defused and life went on.

Legitimate Roles

The roles are an important part of the puzzle. Everyone on the triangle takes on some dramatic role; meanwhile, each person also has some legitimate role that has been abandoned. That's partly why it's such a mess: the ordinary, everyday things aren't getting done.

Let's start with Bill. He has two legitimate roles, office worker and husband, and he's abandoned both of them. Liza has abandoned the role of office worker, and Samantha has abandoned roles of office worker and best friend. People were counting on them to do certain things at certain times. None of the legitimate things got done, and lots of illegitimate things got done instead.

The honest answer is that legitimate roles are boring. Husband is more boring than guy-who's-stepping-out. Best friend is more boring than paramour. Office worker is more boring than jilted lover. Yet the dramatic roles are simply trouble.

Toxic triangles feed on drama; they can be stifled with boredom. Remember, healthy conflict has its boring side. It's not boring to collect a yearly bonus or have a happy marriage, but those long-term pay-offs are a lot more work, with a lot less drama, than the melee that happens in a toxic triangle.

The manager picked two undramatic, legitimate roles—manager and timekeeper—and held to them. Then she insisted that everyone else go back to boring, legitimate roles. No more accusation or re-crimination, no more fire and brimstone, just crunching numbers and moving on. Between that moment and the deadline, she de-manded appropriate behavior and nothing else.

Toxic triangles do melodrama, not real life. Real life is interesting because it's surprising—you can never quite know what people will do next. Once you get the feel of a toxic triangle, there's no surprise to it. There's the inevitable dread of watching a scripted car wreck, but it isn't really a surprise.

Consider the step-mom and the out-of-control teenager. From the step-mom's point of view the ex-wife and kid were both villains, the dad was the victim, and the step-mom tried to be the hero. Of course, she ended up a victim in short order. From the step-son's point of view all grown-ups were villains and he was the victim. The only po-tential heroes appeared as he played the adults against each other. All of this cycled pointlessly but didn't go anywhere.

Finally the step-mom stopped everything. She stopped trying to be hero, villain or victim and turned into a negotiator. She laid out plans, listed goals and refused to be thrown off her stride. By the end, the kid stopped provoking either of the parents and went off and joined the marines. Now there was a role to keep him busy for a while.

Divorced families routinely do toxic triangles, with the roles of victim and villain spinning like a roulette wheel. Somewhere there are appropriate roles, and they're usually abandoned. Mom has a legitimate role which does not include undermining Dad. Dad has a legitimate role which does not include fighting Mom over trivial de-tails or threatening to withhold child support. The kids have a legiti-mate role which does not include pitting Mom and Dad against each other or sabotaging their new relationships.

These are families desperately in need of a little boredom.

Meanwhile, if you arbitrarily stop fighting, don't be surprised if your own friends and allies try to goad you back into the fight. A good part of the nation held it against Hillary Clinton that she never took a two-by-four to her own unfaithful Bill. But apart from the thrill of justice run amok, this kind of acting out is very bad for the people involved. The audience may enjoy the drama, but it's awful for the kids.

Roles and Roles

The roles in the triangle are not all fighting roles. Often all that's expected of the hero is to commiserate endlessly and fruitlessly. The victim may have no intention of doing anything about the problem, and bask in the attention. At other times, the hero will step in to punish the malefactor; but in the drama of the moment the hero inevitably goes too far. As soon as the hero oversteps his or her authority or hurts somebody, the hero becomes a villain.

Villains are typically past victims or heroes. Villain can be a very cool role, with a certain Clint Eastwood or Superbitch cachet. Most villains secretly believe they are unappreciated heroes, but it may have been a while since they've checked to see if their behavior matches their self-image.

Many villains privately claim that they are the victim, the wronged one, the decent soul who may not be decent at all but who can make a case for everyone else being a perfect bastard. Actually, victim is one of the most coveted roles on the triangle. Victims are obsessed with how badly they've been treated, so they often see it as only fair that they should take it out on other people. Victims often become abusive themselves or shamelessly take advantage of anyone who comes within reach.

The flaw is that these are all essentially two-dimensional roles; living, complex human beings can't fit into these cardboard cut-outs. Once people act as people—once the Hero makes a stupid mistake, or the Villain gets hurt—the roles change. The only sure thing is that the triangle may make someone happy briefly and everyone miserable sooner or later.

Costs

Victim/Villain cycles are inordinately expensive in human or economic terms. As any Israeli or Palestinian can tell you, it takes a large part of the gross economic product just to keep them going. Not that the cycle will go anywhere—the cost is just for maintenance.

In the workplace these costly cycles undermine morale and wreak havoc on normal professional conducts. Professions with a certain heroic streak can be particularly prone to this, including medicine, social work, law enforcement, teaching or even volunteer groups.

The syndrome may appear in the international NGO or the social worker down the block. The new hire arrives with high hopes as a hero. She sees her clients as victims and society at large as the villain. As she collides with the reality of slow change and the cynicism of her co-workers, she adds her boss and colleagues to the villain list.

After hitting the wall for a while, resentment sinks in. Now her clients are the villains, she's a grudging hero and starting to consider herself a victim. More bitter yet, she starts lashing out at people around her. Clients and colleagues then become victims and the stage is set for a new hero, who this time will take *her* out.

The same pattern plays out in any number of fields. Nurses may start out as heroes, see patients as victims and disease as the villain. Soon doctors become villains, nurses victims, and anyone who will listen to their troubles becomes a hero. Teachers start out as heroes, with kids as victims and ignorance as villain. Soon kids, parents and the administration become villains, the teacher's a victim, and no one's a hero. By that time the cynical teacher's become a villain, the kids feel like victims, and a furious parent will step forward as hero. And so on.

Combine the victim/villain cycle with long-term flooding and you get burn-out.

Burn out particularly afflicts volunteer groups, which is unfortunate since they can least afford the drain on energy and good will.

Healthy volunteers flee. This isn't just because the place has become so unpleasant, but because they literally can't afford to stay.

A technical club on the internet got embroiled in a flame war after a combative fellow joined and got into a nasty battle with the organizers. Some of the fighting was on the public list, while some was in private email. In any case, the newcomer was finally cut off, but the organizers had the poor grace to trumpet it to the general group (I believe the phrase was "Ding-dong, the witch is dead"). Since most had no idea any fight was going on, this created quite a stir.

In no time at all the triangle was set. The old guard were villains for cutting out the new guy, or the new guy was a villain for hounding the organizers. Various allies—trying to be heroes—were ridiculed as fools and sock puppets for taking one side against the other.

Finally, the organizers admitted they hadn't been at their gracious best and re-instated the newcomer—who promptly slammed them on his return. Four separate times the organizers declared the topic dead, and even created a new list just to handle the controversy. Finally, one key organizer declared that he couldn't justify the time and energy and shut down the whole operation: e-mail, website, server, everything.

He'd hit burn-out. He was a normal person pulled into blind behavior, and the harder he struggled the faster he sank. It had started to take over his life, so he quit. Things calmed down once the other members had to scramble to get the technology going again. They were suddenly busy with legitimate tasks and couldn't afford the other stuff. Once they were too preoccupied to give the newcomer attention he left, no doubt to bless a different group.

There are two ways to counteract burn-out in this syndrome: either step off the triangle or consciously fend off flooding. Of course, it's best to tackle both. But be aware, burn-out is best treated with prevention, not cure. Once people are in the depths of burn-out, they may need to leave and not come back.

Stopping the Spin

Add politics to any topic, however boring, and you can get villains and victims. Add math to the uproar and you're likely to stop the spin.

A national coalition was assembling an insurance package; naturally there were regional differences as well as racial, sexual and cultural splits. At one point, an African-American group went back to the central committee and said, "Why is it we people of color are supposed to work with a bunch of white folks?"

One sentence (and 400 years of history) and all the roles were set. From one point of view blacks were victims and whites were villains; from another blacks were villains (inexplicably hostile), and whites were victims (unfairly accused). Of course, the Asians on the committee were insulted as well, but they didn't have time to get a word in.

Either version called out for a hero. In a wonderful bit of symmetry, both heroes stepped forward simultaneously and locked horns with each other.

The meeting (which still had business to conduct) was rapidly turning into a free-for-all. The Chair stepped forward with an excellent idea: He declared both heroes a sub-committee and had them leave the room to fight it out in private. Anyone who wanted to go with them could.

With both heroes out of the room, he got everyone else down to brass tacks: Was the insurance a good deal or not? Everyone crunched numbers, the African-American contingent as well, and they came to a reasonable decision.

The Chair followed the working protocol. First, he refused any dramatic roles, refusing to be hero, victim or villain. He isolated the people who were most eager to fight, and finally he chose a boring, pragmatic role and stuck to it. Consequently he forced everyone else to get pragmatic, too.

The same process can work in a far more explosive situation, such as the small Russian province of Ingushetia where al-Qaeda was moving in. This was an impoverished Muslim region next to deadly Chechnya, which was embroiled in a civil war. Gen. Ruslan Aushev was governor, a Muslim who had fought for the Russians in Afghanistan. He knew very well how bad it could get if the war in Chechnya spread to his province.

The Russian government had virtually no funds to help, but were willing to send troops. Aushev, however, knew that would only inflame the situation. Instead, he dismantled the triangle.

Refuse to make heroes, villains or victims. When young men were known to be fighting with rebels in Chechnya, Aushev gave orders their families weren't to be harassed. When they returned, the fighters themselves weren't to be arrested. Aushev didn't need any more martyrs.

For every dramatic role there is a boring, legitimate role that isn't getting done. Go do it. Aushev spoke with the families of young militants and urged them to get their sons settled and married. He got communities to help them build houses and purchase livestock, taxis and trucks. He recruited them to join the police and to help build a new provincial university. He wanted them busy and making something of their lives.

Some people will never give up the fight. Isolate them. Well-financed extremists had set up radical schools and mosques to recruit young men. Aushev met with local elders and asked their permission to close these places. Police then escorted the recruiters out of the country.

It worked. Aushev blocked al-Qaeda peaceably in one of the most explosive corners of the world.

The Audience

Triangles are typically audience fights, staged publicly to play for a crowd. Consciously or not, the main parties work the audience. While treacherous, actually this gives the onlookers a good deal of power, especially if they withhold their approval.

Consider the Oklahoma City bombing. It started back at Waco, where David Koresh was the villain, the kids in the compound were the victims, and the FBI was the hero. But the compound exploded and suddenly Koresh was the victim and the FBI was the villain. Then Timothy McVeigh, a militia man, stepped in as avenging hero.

When McVeigh blew up the federal building he became the villain, the dead were the victims, and the rescue workers became the heroes. (As a tangent, some idiots played hero by shooting at Arab-Americans, who had nothing to do with anything.)

The triangle stopped when the heroics came down to rescue workers and medical teams who just did the grueling work. There were no more flashy shoot-outs, just slow, hard work.

Without shoot-outs the militia men no longer looked like heroes or victims, but more like neurotics in camouflage. Their audience turned away from them. The audience may have looked like non-players, but actually the militia depended on their tacit approval. People stopped letting them train on their land, stopped buying them beers. They stopped talking to them when they saw them in town and started crossing to the other side of the street.

False heroes need an audience. Real heroes will still grind through the work, whether or not anyone is watching. The drama queens can't handle it.

If you are called on as audience in such a fight, your most powerful move can be to look bored or walk away. If it's the family fight at Thanksgiving or a pointless office brawl, vote with your feet. Audience involvement will make any triangle more explosive, while boredom or disapproval can have a very real dampening effect. Heroes of this type are not prepared for an audience that finds them distasteful or leaves at intermission.

Unexpected Moves

Villains and victims are painfully predictable. You could take any four people off a city bus, and they would be able to tell you that a bombing by Palestinians will be met by retaliation from Israel, which will be met by a bombing from Palestinians followed by retaliation from Israel. Why strangers on a bus should be so much more precognizant than elected world leaders remains a mystery; yet apparently they can see what will happen next, in a way that prime ministers can't.

This predictability adds momentum to the spin. One way to break the spin is to make an unexpected move, preferably in the opposite direction. Embrace someone you're supposed to hate. If nothing else, it startles people.

When bin Laden bombed the towers in New York, he intended to set off a huge toxic triangle that would consume the world in war. The Americans would lash out at Islam everywhere, and Islam, of course, would retaliate.

Instead, there were two immediate, unexpected moves by leaders, which jarred the spin in the opposite direction. George Bush televised a speech from the national mosque in Washington, D.C., and Yassar Arafat was photographed giving blood for New York.

Now, neither of these moves may have been quite sincere, and they might have worked better had they been followed with real policy. But for that moment both leaders did something sound. With momentum spinning towards all-out war, these two threw restraining lines.

Those anchors slowed the fight, which leads to a curious point: people don't wish to be swept away. Small triangles may be entertaining, but a raging triangle is frightening, like plunging down an abyss. At that moment the audience may believe unlikely things, if only to save themselves. Fear of chaos not a bad survival skill, and it took uncommon good sense for these leaders to invoke it.

The same technique works in smaller fights, of course. Frances Hesselbein threw an anchor in the opposite direction when she invited the demonstrators into the air conditioning for iced tea and cookies. Rather than allow anyone to be a villain or victim, she had her staff became host and open up discussions.

Putting it Together

I once was asked to co-chair a committee where there had been bitter bad blood, with public accusations of racism and other ugly stuff. The other chair was a white woman in a long-standing feud with an Asian woman. This fight had gone on for years. I was asked to step in as a hero. We all know what that means.

What was worse, both these women were my elders, which meant I couldn't fight either one. For someone from my background it is unacceptable to disrespect someone of grandmother status, so fighting wasn't an option.

Before the first committee meeting, word had traveled that trouble was brewing. After the meeting, the Asian woman confronted me and said, "Read this!" and thrust a sheaf of papers in my hands.

I had no idea what this was all about, but I knew I was suddenly the enemy. There were six pages, single spaced, and I was flooding so badly I could hardly read the print. Then I glanced up and saw that a circle had formed around us, waiting for blood. My tenure as hero looked to be quite short.

First of all, I had to get rid of the audience, since they would only make things worse. One way to stop the triangle is to find a boring job to do, so I did. I was asked to read the paper, so I stood there and read it—all six pages, single spaced. Nothing is more boring than watching someone else read. By the time I looked up again the audience had drifted away and only my Asian elder was left, glaring at me.

I'd managed to get past some of my flooding, but I still couldn't make sense of what I'd been handed. Words broke off mid-sentence; sentences started out of nowhere. English didn't seem to be an issue, but I couldn't understand what she was trying to say.

Breathing slowly, I tried a different approach. Since I couldn't follow the argument, I thought of what would be most difficult for me to take in. I have a logical mind and have the most trouble with writing that's free-form or amorphous. Well, this writing was amorphous but I could sketch out broad philosophical trends. Could it be philosophy? I looked up and asked if she were a philosopher.

Suddenly she lost the glare and looked away. She said, "I have taken several philosophy courses at University."

I looked back at the paper, scanning for patterns. The line breaks, the free-form sentences—Could it be poetry? So I asked. Her face melted. She said, "It is written in haiku form."

So that was it! I was expecting a position paper with bullet points and what I'd been handed was a giant haiku. She must have spent an enormous amount of time on that.

I said "You know, for our presentation, we'll have people coming in from all sorts of places, different points of view. It would be good to have something to bring them together, so we could all start out from the same place. Would you be willing to write a poem for us? Would you be our poet?"

The fight was over. Gone. My Asian elder had an honorable role as poet, while I had a role as chair, not hero. My white elder got to stop being villain or victim and enjoy the presentations in peace.

The Asian woman wrote a beautiful poem and sat back, having performed her job well. The fight with the co-chair vanished. That was good, because the white woman died about nine months later. At the time no one knew there was anything wrong, but it meant that the weeks she had left were her own, not caught up in that fierce, bitter acrimony.

Unusually Poor Results

Going back to the problem of toxic triangles fueled by scandal, it's striking that the young manager handled her adulterous up-roar so much more effectively than the U.S. Congress. Granted there was less of an audience, but Congress applied huge sums of money and some of the finest minds in the nation. Yet Congress became so bogged down in drama that the bombing of Serbia looked suspiciously like a sideshow. The conflict didn't just distract a department, it virtually stopped the U.S. Capital.

And exactly what was the point of all that? The Republicans didn't have impeachment law on their side or the necessary votes to force the issue. So why drag the rest of the country through a futile, sordid mess?

Remember: level three conflict seeds the next cycle, and victims and villains seed the next fight. The ill-will lasted to the following election, which was narrowly won by the younger George Bush. However you may feel about how George W. has performed, he was elected as the least intelligent candidate since Dan Quayle. Given the depth and breadth of the Republican Party, he wasn't exactly the pick of the litter.

Republicans, as a group, are generally sharp, well-educated, and markedly ambitious. Agree with them or not, they form an extremely high-caliber field. So what happened to the smart Republicans?

Consider another toxic triangle: Clarence Thomas and Anita Hill. Both sides went whirling through victims and villains, with the black audience weighing in to defend Clarence Thomas. And what did they get for it? Clarence Thomas as a Supreme Court judge. For life.

Clarence Thomas was hardly the most gifted black jurist available. He was primarily known as a government bureaucrat. Even narrowing the field to conservatives, he was hardly the sharpest guy around. So what happened to everyone else?

Toxic triangles yield remarkably poor results. Intelligent people do stupid things and allies hurt themselves to get nothing in return. The audience snaps out of it later, like coming out of a trance. We did what? For whom? Why did we do that and what were we thinking of?

Brains turn off in the toxic triangle. Victims and villains are the pornography of problem-solving, cheap crowd-pleasers that grab audience share and choke out legitimate discussion. Worse, it polarizes debate when different sides desperately need to talk to each other. Intelligent people end up with simple-minded solutions that defy explanation in the cold light of day.

The same factors can be seen in a hundred other chronic disputes, over water rights or product development or environmental suits. As the triangle spins, people hammer at each other without ever stopping to check what they're doing. Even wolves get cast victims or villains, and they're not: for better or worse, they're just wolves.

High Stakes, Big Losses

Rounds of victim and villain can be played for extremely high stakes. In the early sixties we nearly lost the planet to it.

During the Cuban missile crisis, the roles were: Khrushchev as villain, Kennedy as hero and the threatened West as victim. Of course, from the opposite point of view Kennedy was the villain, Khrushchev was the hero and the Cubans were the victims.

As is so often the case, the real issue had nothing to do with all this. Americans had placed short-range missiles in Turkey, where they could strike Russia without appearing on their early warning radar. In retaliation, the Russians wanted short-range missiles in Cuba, tit for tat.

Kennedy found out about the Cuban plan and put the American military on alert. During the stand-off Kennedy assembled an armada the size of the D-Day invasion of Europe, with 180,000 American troops prepared to invade Cuba. It was a massive hero gesture, matched by Russian hero thunder.

However, the two hero/villains were so busy with each other they failed to notice an outside player made a move. The Cubans, those little side victims in this battle of titans, had gotten hold of battlefield nuclear weapons. Their plan was to wait until the Americans landed and nuke the entire expedition. That, of course, would trigger World War III, but the Cubans had decided that this was a good day to die and they were prepared to take capitalism with them. They would become heroes, villains and victims simultaneously in a large cloud of radioactive dust. They were about to blow the game off the planet.

Khrushchev knew what the Cubans had in mind, but he couldn't reach his officers to step down the missiles. Americans had blockaded the island and he couldn't get a message through. Finally in desperation, he sent a diplomatic dispatch to Kennedy which was unlike anything he'd sent before. He wrote about "the knot of war... because the more the two of us pull, the tighter that knot will be tied and a moment may come when it will be tied so tight that we will not have the strength to untie it and then it will be necessary to cut the knot, to doom the world to the catastrophe of nuclear war."

The State Department wasn't sure what to make of the dispatch; they'd never heard a Soviet premiere talk like this before. It wasn't Red Army rhetoric; they weren't sure what it was. Still, a few people had a sense that Khrushchev was trying to say something important. Unsure, Kennedy held off on the command to invade. Step by step, Kennedy and Khrushchev backed off their positions. Khrushchev withdrew the missiles from Cuba and Kennedy quietly took the missiles out of Turkey.

Basically, both sides frightened themselves back to problem-solving and began doing the things that responsible people do when they're in charge of a country. Neither leader became a saint, but their behavior changed markedly. They toned down their rhetoric, opened lines of communication by installing a hot line between the White House and the Kremlin, and went back to practical give and take. Within nine months they had gone from the brink of holocaust to signing the first nuclear arms treaty.

All sides had taken their hero roles seriously and very nearly blew the works. You and I are alive today because they managed to snap out of it. If they hadn't, they would have gone down in history as the world's biggest villains, or perhaps as victims along with the rest of the vaporized population.

Guardianship

Like Khrushchev and Kennedy defending their nations, heroes often sincerely believe they are guardians of some sacred trust. It could be a country, a business, a non-profit or a religion. The more the guardians believe in the cause, and the more emotionally charged the atmosphere, the more likely it is that the guardians will destroy what it is they hold in trust.

You have seen this happen in your own life. You have watched the guardians of a family, a heritage, a company or an institution self-destruct and take their charge with them. This wasn't done from lack of caring. As the saying goes, they seemed to love not wisely but too well. That insight struck Othello *after* he'd killed his beloved.

Sometimes, timing is everything. Kennedy and Khrushchev came within 72 hours of destroying both Russia and America, both capitalism and communism. Yet just before that irrevocable point they paused and changed profoundly.

I think a bond happens at the moment. Kennedy and Khrushchev had become one another, fighting so fiercely not because they were opposite but because they had become so frighteningly alike, mirror images out of control. When Kennedy was killed, it appeared that Khrushchev was genuinely sad, and for good reason. There was no one else on earth who had been through what they'd been through, and no one else who would ever understand.

Not everyone pulls out of it. Families are destroyed; businesses go under. Religions are disgraced by the religious and countries laid waste by their own patriots. Organizations are ripped apart by the people who care about them most.

We watch these things happen and we live with the damage every day. But when we're involved ourselves we don't stop to think that it may not be necessary. We don't realize when we've stepped into their shoes, when we have become the guardians and are about to destroy what we love best; that the short-term thrill will have long-term costs, and no one will thank us for acting this way.

What to Remember

- **The villain/victim/hero cycle** drives a fight towards blind behavior. It produces endless, pointless conflicts that can last for generations. It's the psychodrama equivalent of a perpetual motion machine.

- **Once the cycle starts,** roles will change. The hero will become a villain and the villain will become a victim. There's no stopping it. There are no brakes on this thing.

- **The solution** is to get off the triangle.

- **In the midst of the drama** there are appropriate, undramatic roles that aren't getting done. Find your job and go do it.

- **The triangle feeds on melodrama.** It can be starved with boredom.

- **Some people will never give up the fight.** Isolate them.

- **One hero role** is to be sympathetic and commiserate endlessly. Don't play. Be pleasant, but change the subject or find something else to do.

- **The triangle thrives on an audience.** You can help matters by walking out at intermission.

- **When pushed** towards becoming a villain or victim, it helps to throw an anchor in the opposite direction and extend a gesture towards someone you're supposed to fight. If nothing else, it startles people.

- **The toxic triangle is the pornography of problem solving,** offering cheap thrills that choke out fairness and sane discourse.

- **When villains and heroes** are played for high stakes, sometimes the players manage to shock themselves back to responsible behavior. It doesn't always happen; sometimes they destroy everything. But when it does happen the change can be lasting and profound.

- **Guardianship** requires problem-solving skills: self-control, appropriate behavior, and a willingness to set aside drama. Heroes make terrible guardians.

What Works Where

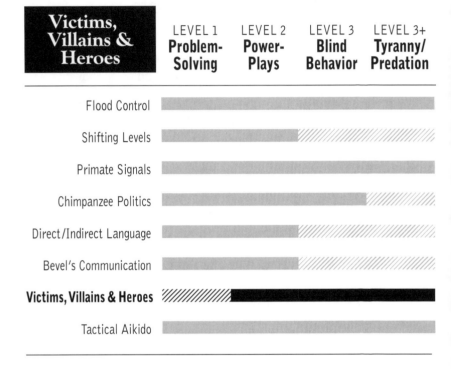

Victims, Villains & Heroes	LEVEL 1 Problem- Solving	LEVEL 2 Power- Plays	LEVEL 3 Blind Behavior	LEVEL 3+ Tyranny/ Predation
Flood Control				
Shifting Levels				
Primate Signals				
Chimpanzee Politics				
Direct/Indirect Language				
Bevel's Communication				
Victims, Villains & Heroes				
Tactical Aikido				

Victims, Villains and Heroes are primarily level three problems. Once in a while a mild case of heroism shows up at level two, but it's apt to deteriorate as people become caught up in drama and blind to their own behavior. It's revealing that villains & victims aren't found at level one; there's too much self-righteousness to allow for healthy problem-solving.

Chapter Ten

Tactical Aikido:
The Principle of Participation

Solutions aren't easy at level three; blind behavior and the vicious circle result in chronic, tenacious conflicts. But apart from working with villains and victims, there's another tactic from Bevel that works very well: the Principle of Participation. It's a legacy of the civil rights campaigns in the deep south, where unarmed people went up against entrenched and violent racists, and won. This technique works at any level, across the chart.

The approach is basically tactical aikido. If someone is too powerful, too headstrong, or is moving with too much momentum, you don't try to stop them at all. It's more like aikido: you step out of the way and keep them moving. You don't oppose them, you go into sync. Perhaps this brings you to resolution or perhaps they throw themselves.

Again, the approach looks deceptively simple:
1) We share common interests.
2) We share common outcomes.
3) The other person has a talent for furthering his or her own interest, and mine.

And what does this have to do with solving impossible conflict? Watch.

A nursing manager worked with a computer geek and they mutually loathed one another. To the nurse the geek was devoid of social skills, came dressed like a slob and worse, was barely nineteen and made twice her salary. They were to design a computer system together, but hated each other so badly there was an office pool on which one would quit first.

This manager's career depended on this project, and she couldn't stand to be in the same room with this guy. At wits' end, she tried the principle of participation.

We share common interests: Well, they certainly didn't share an interest in computers, and this kid seemed to have no interest in patients or anything human. However they were both interested in getting the project done, if only so they wouldn't have to work together.

We share common outcomes: They both wanted to see this project succeed, and they both wanted to share in the success.

The other person has a talent for furthering his self-interest and mine: Here the manager broke down. Talent? He couldn't even carry on a conversation.

Then she stopped herself—that wasn't entirely fair. He knew computers and could deal with the technology she loathed. Of course she thought he was a misfit. He even spent his free time reading computer magazines; but she had to admit those same magazines gave him ideas that helped further their project.

The more she thought about it the more she realized that he brought a great deal to the table, almost all of which was technology she wouldn't want to touch. Then the thought occurred to her: "What am I bringing to the table?"

Well, she was the manager, she was the one with people skills. It occurred to her that if he was bringing so much technology to the table, it was only fair that she bring the management skills. That included communication.

Of course, they didn't begin to communicate. So how was she going to fix that?

He clearly couldn't make himself understood in the everyday world and she wasn't about to learn geek. So she walked into their next meeting with sheets of butcher paper and colored markers. He didn't know how to hold a conversation, but maybe he could draw.

She knew he dreaded these meetings as much as she did, so she started out by saying, "Look, I know we haven't gotten along in the past, so I want to try something different. Instead of talking about things, I want you to sketch things for me. We'll keep drawing pictures until we get it right."

It worked. Hey, he was a kid and he liked drawing pictures. And when they got on each other's nerves (which they inevitably did), she was the one who called an end to the meeting, because she was the one with the people skills to know when they'd had enough.

By using the principle of participation, the manager took a crucial leap. She stopped criticizing the kid for the social skills he lacked, and started working with the skills he did have. And she had to be the one to figure it out because there wasn't a chance in the world that he would.

This brought her back to problem-solving, in spite of her exasperation. She got more fair-minded, more flexible and dropped the constant disapproval. Once she got back to solid ground herself, she could work on getting him out of their shared morass.

Think about it. In many conflicts we become so angry at the other side we forget there's anything else to them. Yet any person is multidimensional, a complex mix of pros and cons. We become so focused on their faults that we fail to notice if there's anything in that mix that can help us.

Remember Bevel's statement: We keep expecting other people to be better than we are. This manager expected the geek to get along with her, knowing full well he didn't have the social skills she had. Obviously that approach was never going to work.

Stopping a Spiral

This technique is also good at putting the brakes on a situation that's rapidly spinning out of control.

Edward owned a condo in the city, but he married someone with a house in the suburbs. He gave up his condo to move to the suburbs, but it was a bad real estate market that year and not much better for rentals. However, he finally managed to find someone to lease the place, a young single woman named Ann.

A few months after Ann moved in, Edward got a call from an old neighbor. The neighbor complained that Ann had gotten drunk the night before and had a screaming fight with her boyfriend. Her boyfriend had thrown her out in the hall and she had woken up the building by screaming obscenities and bashing on the door. The neighbor reported a good deal of damage to the door and could only wonder what the rest of the apartment looked like.

Edward was alarmed to say the least. It sounded like he had rented his condo to a drunk who was already trashing the place. He didn't have time to drive back to the city every time she decided to slug it out with her boyfriend. So Edward called Ann to ask her just what was going on.

Ann immediately went on the defensive. She accused the neighbor of being a busybody and insisted there was no damage to the apartment. In fact, she couldn't hurt the apartment; it was already a dump when she moved in.

Edward indignantly pointed out the apartment was fine when she rented the place. What's more, he had lived there himself and he was not a slob.

By now they were both flooding and yelling at each other. The only thing that got Edward to stop was the realization that he was on his car phone and he was paying for this insanity at seventy five cents a minute. He told Ann he was losing the signal and he'd talk to her later, and got off the line.

What a mess. Edward and Ann had just signed a one year lease and this was not a good start to a business relationship. He didn't want a solid year of this. He couldn't afford to have her move out and he certainly couldn't afford to have her evicted. So somehow, he was going to have to turn this around.

He tried Bevel's Principle of Participation.

We share common interests. He wanted a renter and she wanted to rent. They both had an interest in making it a nice place. Granted, he had moved out without painting the place, but it was still in his interest to have the place nice.

We share common outcomes. He wanted a stable tenant who would stay, and she surely must not want to move again after just a month. They both probably wanted peace. She probably wanted Edward not to bother her, and Edward wanted to not have to bother her.

Ann has a talent for furthering her own interest and Edward's. Well, Ann was certainly good at sticking up for herself; that was a talent to be reckoned with.

Also, Ann had so far paid her rent on time, even a day or two early to allow for the mail. Edward had other friends who had tenants and he knew this was not something to take for granted.

Also, Ann seemed genuinely upset that the apartment was not up to her standards. Maybe Ann had something there. He had moved out in a hurry and when he thought about it, he hadn't painted for several years. Perhaps Ann was right that the place needed some work. Maybe she'd be willing to help with that.

Edward thought it over, especially the part about his not bothering her and her not wanting to be bothered. As a matter of fact, the neighbor down the hall was a busybody, and Edward had seen him start fights between other people in the building. Edward decided to call a different neighbor and double-check the story. The second neighbor gave a much tamer rendition, though he'd also noticed scratches on the door paint.

Edward thought it over and called Ann back with his flooding under control. Ann was ready for a fight, but he quickly apologized for confronting her without first checking his facts.

Being set to fight, she was taken aback by the apology. She stammered a bit and said that she could understand his position and that there really wasn't any trouble with the door. Besides, the place wasn't that bad, it just needed some scrubbing.

Rather than get into the state of his housekeeping, Edward asked what she thought about the paint. He hadn't thought about painting the place—would she be willing to do it, if he bought the paint? They worked out a deal where Ann would chose the paint and send Edward paint chips, Edward would buy the paint and Ann would do the painting. The scratches on the door were repaired without anyone ever mentioning it.

Notice again that once a dialogue happened, Ann made an unexpected concession. The relationship since has been peaceful and respectful; the brawl was not repeated.

Overlooking a Useful Opponent

Sometimes people fail to notice a good use for the other side even when it's presented wrapped in ribbon.

The director of an arts council had to decide the future of an eight story arts center in what had become a trendy and expensive part of town. There was room for about 50 individual artists and organizations, ranging from a small opera company to some elderly amateur potters.

The space was owned by the city and enjoyed subsidized rents. Getting in was a haphazard process—usually whoever happened to be around the day a space came vacant became the person to get the space.

The problem was that a number of the artists who rented space were not exactly world-class talents. They were local residents and not about to set the world on fire. The new director saw that this space had the makings of a first-rate facility that could attract international artists for residencies.

The local artists weren't thrilled with this approach. They didn't like hearing their work described as second-rate, and they weren't about to be thrown out for some newcomer with a nose ring.

Meanwhile, the arts budget got sliced at city hall, where the arts council was considered an anachronism. In a city-wide prioritization of funds, the arts council came in last.

With big cuts on the horizon, the arts director informed the artists that they would all be facing a 10% rent increase. They were outraged, but the director wasn't sure if he minded or not. He thought if some of the lower quality artists would move out they might have room for better talent. However, the untalented artists were not the ones about to move. The talented ones would run out of money first, while the wealthy amateurs held on to their leases.

The director was fielding complaints and waiting for the ax to fall, when, without warning, a group of local artists went over his head and stormed a city council meeting. The artists got into a yelling match with the budget committee and reduced the meeting to bedlam.

The arts director was mortified. This wasn't the kind of image he was trying to project and he re-doubled his efforts to get these people out. But a funny thing happened on the way to the budget cut. This was a staid, respectable town; they didn't have people yelling and screaming at city hall. The city council was shocked; they didn't know anyone cared that much about art. Not wanting to face that kind of scene again, they restored most of the arts funding and the renters got only a 5% increase. Everyone could stay.

The director, however, saw this as proof that there was no living with these people and they really had to go. But he got that exactly wrong. Not only did these people make bad enemies, they were clearly valuable allies.

Look at it according to Bevel: They shared common interests in art and the community, even if their standards weren't the same. They shared common outcomes in seeing the art center continue and thrive.

As for their talents: they were rude, disruptive and ignored proper channels—*and got the budget restored when everyone else had given up.* Perhaps they couldn't hold their own as professional artists, but they were formidable fund-raisers who kept the center from collapsing. That was worth something.

They weren't great artists, but they were an ace in the hole. This center had fifty spaces; there was room for some marginal talent and the rabble-rousers had proven their value. Certainly the budget committee didn't want to face them again.

This was not the talent the director expected, but it was undeniably real. Reconsidering, the director had them grandfathered into the new agreement. Future artists would be admitted through a juried show, but the rabble-rousers had their leases guaranteed. If one of the lesser talents moved out the space would pass to a juried talent, but it would only change by natural attrition. Perhaps it was wise to keep some fiery old-timers on hand, just in case.

Natural Gifts

Baron von Clausewitz, the military theorist, realized that it wasn't enough to focus on an opponent's weakness. The opponent could always improve a weakness, protect it or turn it into a strength. Instead, von Clausewitz suggested to focus on their strengths, because an opponent could never abandon a strength. The strength was an essential part of who they were.

The question is how to use that strength to one's own advantage.

I once had a particularly bright, capable student, who wouldn't complete her assignments. She was a natural-born leader but worked at a clerical job, thought all managers were idiots and had her peers at work united in an us-against-them deadlock.

For homework she'd start a technique with these managers, go so far, decide, "But of course they're just jerks," and stop dead. And complain. If you have a complainer who's a natural born leader, you have a real problem on your hands. From her papers I had to pity her managers. She must have given them a lot of sleepless nights.

However, my main concern was with her effect on my class. Because she was such a leader, a circle would form around her with everyone complaining about their own bosses. You don't get college credit for complaining, and I had to get them back on track. More to the point, I had to get this smart, capable woman to start performing up to her abilities and stop quitting at the first annoyance.

I gave her some latitude at first, hoping she would come around. That didn't work. When she turned in yet another assignment where she quit mid-stream, I attached a note to her paper. I explained that I thought she was extremely intelligent, a gifted leader, and there were people with half her ability who were doing better than she was. She was getting left behind, and what did she plan to do about that?

I think this came as a cold-water shock. She may have been about to bridle, but then she listened to a string of other people describe ingenious solutions to the same assignment she'd dropped cold. And she realized the class *was* passing her by.

I'd pegged her right: a natural leader can't *not* lead. To give her credit, she did a complete about face; I don't think it took her twenty minutes. Her final project was detente with one of the managers she'd previously driven to distraction.

Now, in this case the pieces to the puzzle were not what they appeared to be:

We share common interests: We shared an interest in conflict management, at least as far as that class.

We share common outcomes: Here's where it gets tricky. You might think that she wanted an end to her problems with managers and that I might have been able to help her with that. I'm not so sure. She was so competent I think she could have worked things out with the managers whenever she wanted. She didn't need my help to do it.

Instead, the common outcome was for her to behave as a smart, able leader. She liked her ability, but I think leading came so naturally to her that she took it for granted. I also liked her ability to lead, but I wanted her to lead in a constructive direction.

I also wanted her to be the most she could be. I don't know if she started out thinking of herself as possessing a first-rate mind, but soon she was trying this on for size.

She had a talent for furthering her own interests and mine: She couldn't *not* lead. She could lead the class into endless complaints, or she could show them what an impressive turn-around looked like. She was more than capable of doing either one. It was a thrill to watch her drop the complaining and gather her life in her own hands.

I imagine that in the past a number of managers had tried to bully her into doing what they wanted. Poor saps.

The Value of Truth

I had to jolt this student to get her attention, and there are few things more shocking than the truth. Flattery won't do; there's nothing shocking about flattery no matter how well it's done. And besides, she was too smart to be lied to.

I genuinely respected her and I was telling the truth when I said she was capable of much more than what she'd been doing.

Now, you may wonder what I might have done if she weren't particularly intelligent, capable or a natural leader. Then I would've had to identify the talents she did have. You can't get a lasting solution with this technique by lying.

Lying undermines its own foundation. Adults sense when they're being lied to; children sense when they're being lied to. Even dogs know when they're being lied to. Why insult the other person and risk embarrassing yourself?

True statements carry weight and power that the most appealing lie can't match. I told her she was intelligent and a leader, and that more was expected of her. She looked around, could see that was true and proceeded to act accordingly. But what if she looked around and couldn't find the qualities I was depending on. She couldn't make bricks out of straw. How could she build a sound structure on an imaginary foundation?

Too often we try to build up someone's self-esteem by flattery. This backfires. Telling people that they've done a good job when they haven't, or are doing fine when they're failing miserably, is insulting and sabotages genuine integrity. Lies can't build character, they only build complacency.

This is not to say you shouldn't be encouraging and shore up confidence when things look bleak. We've all learned that sometimes you tell yourself you can do something, and then go out to do it before you remember that you can't. That's not lying: that's learning about growth and potential, testing the waters of possibility. That's very different from empty flattery.

Consider the spot I was in with the Asian elder who was furious with me. It wasn't inspiration that I asked her to write a poem—it was the Principle of Participation. I looked for her talent that could benefit both of us and the solution jumped out at me.

Now: what if the Asian woman had been a rotten poet, and I had just pandered to her vanity? Was she to stand up in public and be a pretend poet? How long would it have been before she realized I was stringing her along? And what would be the price I'd pay once she realized her good will had been betrayed and I'd set her up in public?

Lies de-stabilize things. She was a good poet, and that was the obvious choice. But if she weren't, I would have needed to find another talent. She had lived a long life; she had other talents. It would have been my job to find them.

The Principle of Participation works on hard cases, so it has to withstand a lot of pressure. Lies aren't strong enough to bear the weight. It's like thinking it's too hard to lay a foundation with concrete, so instead you build on cardboard. Cardboard might be easier to work with, but you'll also find that the building caves in.

David & Goliath

Like aikido, the Principle of Participation works when the other side is so large and strong they simply can't be defeated.

There was a renovation contract that turned into a project from hell. It was a lakeside mansion owned by one of the richest and most powerful lawyers in the state, and more things went wrong than can be listed here. But the worst of it was the flooring subcontractor. The floor was wrong, and aside from the ruined tile a lot of other things couldn't be finished without the floor. The family was scheduled to move in soon, and the phone calls escalated from ominous to openly threatening.

The general contractor was in no position to take on this lawyer. The project had been severely underbid and a lawsuit would finish off the company. When the contractor confessed that a lawsuit would probably bankrupt the firm, the lawyer just offered to sue them all personally. This was exasperating. The contractor was willing to do anything to fix this, but he couldn't control the flooring subcontractor. Meanwhile the lawyer was sharpening his knives.

Desperately casting around for a solution, the contractor worked on the Principle of Participation. By that time, all problems had been resolved except for the flooring.

They shared common interests/ outcomes: Both parties wanted the project done. The client didn't want to spend any more money, and the contractor was willing to absorb the rest of the costs if he could just get out from under the job. They both wanted the client happy and off the phone.

The other side has a talent for furthering his own interest and mine: This was an aggressive and well-connected lawyer who was furious and ready to act. Very well. The contractor offered to hire the lawyer's firm to sue the flooring company.

The lawyer seemed taken aback. After thinking it over he declined the case, citing conflict of interest. He still reserved the right to sue everyone involved, but in practice he stopped beating up on the contractor. The threatening phone calls stopped. The lawyer would make progress checks with the general contractor and discuss ways to bring pressure on the flooring guy, but he was no longer on the attack—at least not towards the contractor.

The contractor had to be truthful to make this work. If this were merely a ploy, that lawyer would have had him for lunch. But the contractor really had done everything possible and had nothing to hide. The lawyer could finally hear that and direct the pressure where it was needed.

The Principle at Level Three

Now, all of these cases so far, no matter how difficult, still involved people who were able to change their behavior. They could shift back to problem-solving, so they did. It's the classic solution of level two.

But what if they're truly stuck and can't get back to problem-solving? They are who they are, they have no self-awareness and no ability to grow better overnight.

The Principle of Participation works just as well.

There was a custody mediation during a divorce. The husband was an alcoholic, a binge drinker who got paid on Friday and drank most of his paycheck on the spot. The problem was that the judge assigned joint custody and mandated that the father was to pick up his little girl after work on Friday. Hell would freeze over before this judge would change his decision.

The mother was beside herself. She did not want her daughter in a car with a drunk driver. The father swore he could quit drinking any time and thought the mother was being ridiculous. Rather than argue through an invincible case of denial, the mediator came up with a solution: The father would pick up the daughter on Friday, and if the mother was concerned she could ask him to drive to a police station and get a Breathalyzer test. If the test was negative, no problem. Otherwise, he had to wait until he sobered up to get the little girl.

The father thought this was fine, as long as he could have the mother tested, too. The mom agreed and they both signed.

Now, you may wonder what possessed the father to sign this agreement. He'd been getting blind drunk every Friday for years. But think in terms of Bevel:

They shared common interests: Both parents loved this little girl.

They shared common outcomes: They both wanted the best for their child. Both parents wanted her safe and both parents agreed that she should never ride with a drunk driver.

The other side has a talent for further his own interest, and the child's: Perversely, the father had two talents, his love and his denial. He really believed he could stop drinking at any time, and believed it so completely that he signed the agreement without a second thought.

This was a fine agreement. If driving sober, the father could have his daughter. If not, the little girl was protected.

Now, you might object that this was taking advantage of the man, nearly assuring he wouldn't get to see his daughter. Not at all. He could come get her sober. He could even do it drunk, as long as someone else was driving. And if he couldn't stay sober long enough to pick up his daughter, then maybe—just maybe—it might dawn on him that something was wrong.

Rather, this agreement spoke to the best in this man. He may have been a drunk but he was also a father who loved his little girl. The drunk may not have known the right way to behave, but the loving father did. It was the loving father who signed that agreement, overruling the interests of the drunk. That's what loving fathers do.

Involuntary Cooperation

Someone does not have to like you to make this technique work; cooperation isn't necessarily voluntary. This tactic is so effective it can work even when the other side doesn't like you, doesn't wish to help you, and knows exactly what you have in mind.

A case in point was the Selma campaign, where King, Bevel and Nash faced the white establishment and Sheriff Jim Clark, who was a hard core racist and as mean as a snake. King intended to stage peaceful demonstrations for voting rights, while letting Sheriff Clark showcase his personality before the press. However, King's attache was stolen on his way to Selma and his plans ended up with the Alabama authorities. Seeing what King had in mind, they determined not to let Jim Clark act out, at least not in front of the cameras.

The tactic nearly worked, but King and his aides really understood Clark: the sheriff couldn't *not* act out. He couldn't *not* be vicious. Finally, Clark shoved his handlers aside and went after the marchers full bore. The culmination was the onslaught against praying protesters at the Pettus Bridge, which made headlines around the world.

This became an international incident, embarrassing the nation in the midst of the Cold War. President Johnson stepped in with a voting rights bill, which opened up voting throughout the South.

Look at it through Bevel's principle:

We share common interests: Both sides focused on Selma, Alabama.

We share common outcomes: Both sides wanted peace and calm to return to Selma. They had different ideas of what a just peace looked like, but both sides wanted the fighting over.

The other side has a talent for furthering their interest and ours: Jim Clark had a talent for violence. He would do anything to any black person at any time, and you could count on him for it. So the civil rights workers put him in a position where his talent would be showcased, not just locally where no one in power would mind, but internationally where the public would be appalled.

Calling for the Gift

Even at level three, the pivotal talent may be a gift or a quality that everyone else has overlooked. The gift may have been there all along, but perhaps no one's ever thought enough of these people to ask for it.

Eliza had an adopted nephew, Jack, who arrived 8 years old and feral, from a deeply troubled home. The officials thought there wasn't much hope for this kid and he was assigned to a special school for behavior disordered children. That was bureau-speak for a holding tank before prison. But Eliza didn't believe these kids were hopeless, not hers nor anyone else's.

One day Jack got into a serious fight on the school bus. A meeting was called with all the parents and guardians, the social worker, the principal, all the big guns. Jack was on the spot; everyone said it was all his fault. Of course, the kids who accused him were there, as well.

Eliza is a big woman, and she sat down at the table and gestured to the social worker to give her a minute. She leaned towards the kids and said, "I'm Jack's guardian. You've probably heard about me. I'm the mean one. Now I want you to tell me *exactly* what Jack did to cause all this, because I'm the mean one, and I'll see to it that Jack answers for it. So tell me *exactly* what happened."

Those kids couldn't fall over themselves fast enough to clear Jack's name. Yes, he'd acted out, but they'd ganged up and baited him because he was the new kid. The adults got the whole truth from everyone, no excuses. Jack got his fair share of the punishment, but he didn't get railroaded or turned into a pariah.

Those kids had a gift: a sense of hoodlum honor. They had integrity and it was high time someone invoked it. They'd protect their own and suddenly Jack had become their own. That had a lot to do with whether or not Jack survived long enough to make it out of that school.

When it Looks Like Nothing Will Work

My mother had had heart surgery and was not a model patient. She had great charm and a serious passive-aggressive streak, and didn't like hospitals one bit. Once she got out of intensive care she wanted to go home and so she refused to eat, take her medication or do any of her exercises. The doctors thought this meant she wasn't feeling well, and wouldn't let her leave until she showed some signs of life. The impasse lasted a good six weeks. Finally my mother decided to cooperate, did everything required and the doctors sent her home. Then she took to her bed, turned the lights off and refused to do another thing.

I was looking after her, and it became my job to get her to do all the things the nurses couldn't get her to do. Worse, she liked having me back home again and the longer she took to recuperate, the longer she'd have me around. My mother thought very long term.

I was already worn out from her hospital stay, and after another month of no cooperation I was starting to lose my mind.

My life and business were going to pieces while I was tending my mother as an invalid, and the tests were quite clear: she was healthy as a horse. I only hope I have her genes, because with an ounce of effort she could have lived forever. As it was, she would hardly get out of bed. I suppose walking out was an option, but this was my mother and I really did care about her, even though I wanted to wring her neck.

I tried everything I could think of to get her to eat or exercise. Nothing worked. There was no talking to her—she could not or would not understand that I was going to lose my business if she kept this up. Finally, in desperation I sat down and worked it out according to Bevel. What I found was sobering:

We shared common interests: Well, I loved her and she loved me, but that seemed to reinforce the trap rather than offer a way out.

We shared common outcomes: Very bad. I couldn't think of an outcome we shared. I wanted her to get back into the swing of things and let me go home. She wanted to stay in bed and have me tend her.

I couldn't think of anything that would bring us together.

She had a talent for furthering her own interests and mine. This was worse. She had many talents, but I couldn't for the life of me see how any of them would get her to take her medicine or let me go home.

This frightened me. The Principle of Participation always works. I felt stunned that I was up against something that even this couldn't handle. But there's a principle from self-defense: If someone has you completely pinned and unable to move, odds are he can't move either. So you stay calm and watch for an opening. Something has to give.

I decided to sleep on it and see what developed.

The next morning I went downstairs to fix breakfast and I noticed something odd about the kitchen. My mother had an intricate system of interlocking pans and lids that she kept in the oven for storage. I'd been baking the night before and I was sure I hadn't put them away—in fact, her system was so intricate I didn't know how. Yet the pans and lids were nowhere in sight. I checked. They were back in the oven, precisely in place.

This rocked me back on my heels. Either there were elves in that house or my mother had gotten up in the night, after I had gone to bed, and put the pans away.

Revelation: I had just discovered an exercise program. Just to see, I baked something that morning and after washing up, left the pans and lids on the counter. I went to do the shopping and when I came back, my mother was still in bed in the dark, and the pans were stacked in their place.

All right. Now I had a plan. I baked dinner that night, washed up and scattered pots all over the kitchen. When I came down in the morning they were neatly put away. I moved a lamp five inches to the left and went to the basement. When I came up again it was precisely back in place. My most devilish moment was when I pulled the laundry out of the dryer, brought it upstairs and draped it all over the living room furniture. Then I ran errands for a few hours. When I came back it was all neatly folded and stacked on the dining room table.

Folding laundry is good for the heart: It moves the arms and ventilates the lungs, just like calisthenics.

I'd found her talent. My mother might have been a helpless old woman waiting to die, but no one was going to mess up her house.

Another way of putting it was that my mother thrived on adversity. I needed to stop being such a good daughter and start annoying her, because that was the only thing that would get her moving again.

I can't tell you exactly when she dropped the charade. Until the day I left she never would do anything in front of me. I might be upstairs and hear her in the laundry, or come into the kitchen just as she was sitting down. But after a while it was an open secret and I could make plans to go home.

This solution had probably been in front of me all along, but I'd been flooding too badly to see it.

There was another aspect to all this. While I got her to engage and start eating again, I never got her to do her heart exercises. Rather than throw myself against that, I thought of Bevel's saying, "We keep expecting other people to be better than we are." My mother had heart problems, but it occurred to me that I was fast approaching middle age and I came from a family where nearly everyone died of heart attacks. So I stopped trying to get her to do her exercises (which was impossible), and put myself on an exercise regime. Whenever I got too frustrated for words, I'd get on the NordicTrack. I stuck with it and didn't gain the thirty pounds that nearly everyone seems to pick up in their forties. It didn't help her any, but it helped me a lot.

Hatred

Now you may suspect that some of these examples tap an underlying goodwill that could ultimately make things turn for the better. Like the confrontation at Selma, many level three conflicts have nothing but bitterness to the core. What then?

I once mediated the case of a business deal gone bad, that had spun wildly out of control. It wasn't a lot of money, but both parties were church ladies and it had come down to pounding on each other's doors at night and threatening each other's kids. It was level three and counting.

As often happens, one would not give up the fight. The other was willing to pay her off, but needed to do it in time payments. Rather than consider the offer, the first one exploded in a full blown rage seizure. She swore that she would get that money if it was the last thing she ever did, if she had to follow her to the ends of the earth. She would get that money or see her in hell.

Time to call a break. I talked to this one in private.

I gave her a moment to come back down, then I quoted her back to herself: "'Follow her to the ends of the earth.' 'If it's the last thing I do with my last dying breath.' Just like Ruth and Naomi: 'Wither thou goeth, I will go.'

"You wake up thinking about her in the morning and go to sleep thinking about her at night. More than you think about your husband, more than you think about your kids.

"You know, there are two great bonding emotions, love and hate, and it seems to me she owns you."

Then I made her an offer. I asked what it was worth to her to never see this woman again. Was it worth waiting on a few hundred dollars?

This was the turning point in the case. We got it wrapped that afternoon.

We share common interests/outcomes: They started out sharing a business deal. By the end, they both would do better if they never laid eyes on each other again.

The other person has a talent for furthering her own self-interest and mine: Her talent in this case was her hatred. Her hatred had enslaved her to the other woman, which was very uncomfortable once it was pointed out. Her hatred had backed her into a corner and it became my job to find a way out.

Level three conflict is ultimately all about power, but as long as this kind of thing continues, the people involved don't have any. They have no freedom, no independence, and are utterly ruled by the person they hate. Any sane captive would claw through stone to be free of something like that.

Political Aikido

Finesse has its place in deflecting power politics. The same principles are in play: instead of opposing overwhelming force, takes what comes at you and put it to use.

The United States had criticized Cuba and demanded that it release its political prisoners. Instead of doing the usual pro-forma dispute, Castro promptly complied by shipping the entire prison population to Florida. Before we knew it, the streets of Miami were awash with Cuban pickpockets and drag queens, courtesy of the State Department. This led to a minor crime wave and improved fashion sense, at least until many of the visitors found a new home in American jails.

You may not like Castro, but you have to admit he has a sense of humor.

President Johnson used a different variation when he, too, simply could not use force. It was when three civil rights workers disappeared in Mississippi. The local police wouldn't press the investigation, claiming that it was all a publicity stunt. The FBI wouldn't investigate, since Hoover ran the bureau as a personal fiefdom and had no love for the civil rights movement. Meanwhile, the press was clamoring and Johnson needed results.

Johnson came to the conclusion that in fact he was dealing with three sovereign states: America, Mississippi and J. Edgar Hoover. The governor of Mississippi, denying any problem, said Johnson was welcome to send someone to look into the matter. Very well. Johnson sent Hoover's bitter rival, the former head of the CIA.

When Hoover learned that his arch-rival was in Mississippi, perhaps to crack the case without him, he promptly dispatched a team of investigators. The FBI found the bodies first.

Johnson identified Hoover's gift: simple, petty jealousy in one of the most powerful men in the nation.

Facing Overwhelming Force

A string of national movements have used tactical aikido to achieve their freedom peacefully, when facing overwhelming odds. While many of these leaders became legends, non-violence does not require sainthood. It can be done by regular people.

Gandhi evicted the British from India, King dismantled Jim Crow in the South, Mandela ended apartheid in South Africa, and the Lithuanians broke free of the Soviet Union. Gandhi, King and Mandela were spiritual icons. Lithuanians just wanted the Russians gone.

Lithuanians had been working on getting the Russians out for the previous fifty years. It hadn't gone well. A local joke was that Lithuania wasn't tiny but was actually the largest country in the world: It had its coastline on the Baltic, its government in Moscow and its population in Siberia.

By the 1990s the television station in Vilnius, the capital, was a center of the liberation movement. One bitter January night Soviet troops seized the station. The population of Vilnius turned out to oppose them. They didn't throw rocks at the tanks in the square (which would have been pointless), but surrounded the tanks and would not go home. The tanks ran over several people; still the crowds didn't attack and didn't go away.

This left the Red Army in a quandary. They were trained to fire on hostile forces, but did not know what to do when faced with a crowd of students, grandmothers and housewives. The commanders tried waiting them out, but the crowd stayed put in the sub-Arctic weather. Finally the tanks withdrew and the Lithuanians took back their television station. It was unclear whether the soldiers refused to fire or if their officers decided not to test their obedience.

Once it became known that the Red Army wouldn't fire on its own civilians, national movements across the country took courage and a chain reaction brought down the Soviet Union.

We share common interests: Both sides focused on the center of Vilnius.

We share common outcomes: Both sides wanted peace and stability, although they had different notions of what that would be.

The other side has a gift for furthering their self-interest and ours: The Red Army was trained as an army of the masses, the strong right arm of the people's will. When put to the test, they could not fire on their own population. Their own ideals are what stopped them.

The Lithuanians didn't pour into that square knowing they would succeed; few knew they were doing what Gandhi would have done. It seems a good many thought they probably were going out to get themselves killed. They only knew that they wanted the Russians to leave, and that they would do whatever it took to make that happen.

What to Remember

Bevel's Principle of Participation consists of three steps:
1) We share common interests.
2) We share common outcomes.
3) The other side has a talent for furthering his or her own interests, and mine.

- **For top level conflict** this technique works extremely well , and not many things do. It's extremely effective at lower levels as well.

- **Seeing the worst of the other side** is a normal consequence of long-term conflict. Yet that is only a partial picture. If a solution could be found there you would have already found it. This technique gives you a chance to examine good points as well, to see if anything can be worked with.

- **When searching for the talent,** be honest with yourself and the other side. Don't flatter, don't make excuses, just work with the truth. This technique can take a lot of strain, but if you build on lies you invite collapse.

- **When an opponent is too strong to defeat** this is the tactic of choice. Instead of fighting their strength, *use* their strength. Instead of boxing, try aikido. Don't push. Pull.

- **The other person doesn't need to wish to help you** to benefit you just the same.

- **If you cannot find a useful talent** or common outcomes, calm down and wait. Keep your eyes open. Somewhere there's an opening, and if you stay calm you can find it.

- **Moral enlightenment** isn't required. Tactical aikido is simply good strategy.

What Works Where

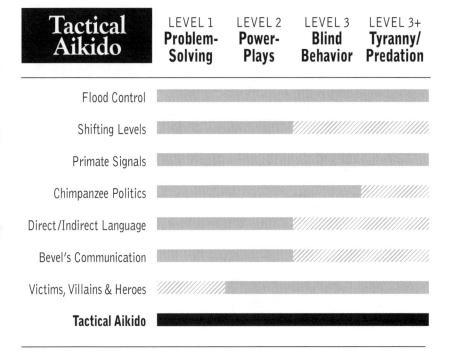

Tactical Aikido	LEVEL 1 Problem-Solving	LEVEL 2 Power-Plays	LEVEL 3 Blind Behavior	LEVEL 3+ Tyranny/Predation
Flood Control				
Shifting Levels				
Primate Signals				
Chimpanzee Politics				
Direct/Indirect Language				
Bevel's Communication				
Victims, Villains & Heroes				
Tactical Aikido				

Tactical Aikido will work at any level of conflict. You'll need to find the point of leverage, but once you do that you can move the earth.

Poststcript

As I said at the start of this book, this work is a piece of my overall conflict model. For instance, the three categories listed cover the range of everyday life, but there are additional categories beyond that range. There's a fourth category of deeply pathological behavior, where messiah/ monsters like Milosevic or bin Laden blur the line between genius and insanity. At the healthy extreme there are rare, gifted leaders like Gandhi or Mandela, whose behavior is so advanced that it can't exactly be called conflict, even though they're consistently found at the center of a storm. Their behavior charts out beyond level one, moving beyond rationality to wisdom, beyond stoicism to a strange fearlessness. These are all worth knowing about, but they're more than can be covered in a single book.

But I wanted to leave with a word about working the part of the puzzle that was covered in this book. When describing these cases sometimes people say that they couldn't possibly come up with solutions themselves, could never think up such things on the spot. Of course it's normal to feel frozen in a conflict and normal to have no idea what to do, especially once flooding has kicked in. But in practice, you don't need to think faster. You need to slow down the fight.

While a given argument may happen very quickly, most conflicts take place over weeks, month, even years. In fact, these fights are so redundant you'll have a dozen opportunities for a second chance. The same fight happens over and over; you have all the time in the world. You can take a break, think things over and come back whenever you feel like it. The same fight will be waiting for you, as timeless as if you hit the 'pause' button on the VCR.

The important thing isn't the quick reply; the important thing is to try something new. It doesn't matter if you don't know what to do. It's conflict: by nature it's murky and confusing. The secret is to have a few basic skills and the willingness to try something new.

Here is one final story. One woman had a father with a tremendous temper, who came from the old country tradition of the man who ruled the house with an iron fist. Naturally this went over very well with his modern, Americanized daughter. Yet he was like his father and his grandfather before him; he had few social skills, no friends and barely knew how to talk except for yelling at people.

One day the daughter came back from traveling and realized that her father had become an old man. He wasn't going to last much longer and she made a decision to get to know him before he died. She did love him, though she wasn't sure why, and she decided to work out whatever still needed to be settled between them because she didn't want to spend the next twenty years in therapy.

So this daughter set about coming to terms with her father. To start off, they fought. He would yell at her and she would yell back that he couldn't talk to her that way. They got into a series of tremendous rows which exhausted both of them and went absolutely nowhere.

Now, this daughter had watched her father spend decades yelling at people and making a mess of things, and yet here she was yelling at him and being puzzled that things didn't work any better for her. If she didn't yell back she didn't know what to do, yet so far all she had accomplished was to become like him. They were both squarely in their blind spots.

The daughter finally realized she had no idea how to make headway with the old guy, and had never seen anyone else handle him either. All she knew was that she had to try something different because yelling back and forth obviously wasn't working.

One day the daughter was in the living room talking with her parents and a few family members when her father suddenly went ballistic. The room promptly emptied out as everyone scattered. As she was leaving, she realized that this was the family pattern: her father would fly into a temper and everyone else would evacuate. Since that was what they had always done, she decided to stay around.

By then her father had moved into the kitchen, where he was storming back and forth and yelling at the walls. So the daughter went in the kitchen and sat down, since that was something else she had never done.

Now the daughter was sitting at the kitchen table with her father yelling at the cabinets; he was so furious he didn't notice she was there. She still didn't know what to do, so she tried to think of something else she had never tried. It occurred to her she'd never tried listening to what he was saying. That didn't sound promising but she didn't know what else to do, so she tried to follow what on earth he was raving about.

In a bit she managed to piece together that he was angry about the car. She remembered that just before he flew into a rage he had asked her mother how the car was running. The mother had said "OK" and the father went insane.

Now, her father didn't deal well with people but he was very good with machines. Piecing the story together she finally understood that he had put a lot of work into that car and her mother didn't even notice.

Well, that was new. She'd never known there was a reason for him to fly into a rage. Who would have thought it? After a while he began to settle down and started to notice there was someone else in the room. He paused and looked a little embarrassed, and the daughter asked if all this was about the car. He went ballistic again.

Now the daughter could piece out the rest of the story. It had been hot and very difficult, and her mother hadn't even said "Thank you." When he paused again the daughter tried out the idea and asked if that was why he was so upset.

He burst out "Yeah!" and stopped. They both stared at each other. They had never gotten that far before and didn't know what to do.

He was still by the counter so the daughter asked if she could have some salami, and he made her a salami sandwich.

Now, this daughter didn't like salami, but it's Bevel again: Who did she need to be to solve this problem? At that moment she needed to be someone who ate salami. But more than that, she needed to be someone who would try something different even though she didn't know where to begin. And of all things what worked was to listen to the old guy.

The answer still hinged on supply and demand: since no one ever listened to her father, listening turned out to be in high demand. Now, you might think that if he really wanted to be listened to he might have tried talking like a reasonable person. That's a valid point, but her father didn't have those social skills: she did. And she wasn't doing this for his benefit, but for her own. So if she wanted to have this problem solved, she had to be the one to do it.

Now her father didn't magically learn how to get along with people after this. It was still rough going. But she learned something else about supply and demand. On the occasions he would manage to speak with her like a human being, the daughter would send him a card about how good it was to talk with him. It turned out no one ever sent her father letters. He didn't have friends and besides, who would correspond with someone who behaved like that?

This triggered more supply and demand. It turned out her father loved getting letters. He would carry them around with him and talk to them when he was angry (which was often). She had finally found a way to get through to her father, and they managed to build a relationship before he died.

Throughout this whole adventure she was finding her way through the unknown. She had never seen anyone walk this trail before. Of course there may have been other solutions, but she wasn't going to find any of them until she gave up her old patterns.

Solving conflict is not about having all the answers. Solving conflict is about finding your way in the dark sometimes, making an educated guess and taking the next step into the unknown. This is what first got us out of the caves, got us fire and bread and the polio vaccine.

It's the great human endeavor, finding your way in the dark. You'll have good company.

What Works Where

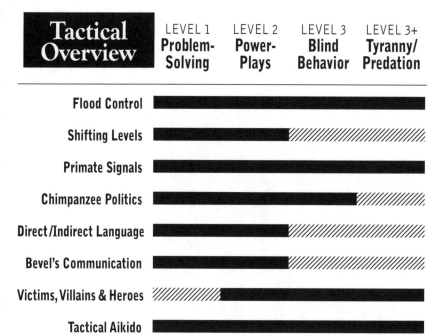

Tactical Overview	LEVEL 1 Problem-Solving	LEVEL 2 Power-Plays	LEVEL 3 Blind Behavior	LEVEL 3+ Tyranny/Predation
Flood Control	████	████	████	████
Shifting Levels	████	████	////	////
Primate Signals	████	████	████	████
Chimpanzee Politics	████	████	████	////
Direct /Indirect Language	████	████	////	////
Bevel's Communication	████	████	////	////
Victims, Villains & Heroes	////	████	████	████
Tactical Aikido	████	████	████	████

Endnotes

Chapter 4

Pg.53 " *'But now, Sam, you know dat all he do is big-belly round....'*"—Hurston, Zora Neale. <u>Their Eyes Were Watching God</u>.

Pg 60 *"The great apes have a solution, which for lack of a better word, can be referred to as leadership posture."*—The formal term in primatology is 'dominance posture,' but that term has entirely different connotations for humans.

Pg 90 *Lincoln photo*— Credit: Library of Congress, Prints & Photographs Division, FSA/OWI Collection, [reproduction number, e.g., LC-USF34-9058-C].

Chapter 5

Pg. 68 *"There was pride in the work and how each cowboy done it..."*— James, Will, "The Breed of 'Em", from Cow Country, 1927. Collected in <u>Literature</u>, McDougal, Littell, Evanston, IL, 1987.

Pg. 69 *"In that book Frances Hesselbein, one of the most respected managers in the nation, described her management system..."*— Helgesen, Sally. <u>The Female Advantage: Women's Ways of Leadership</u>, Doubleday, New York. Pg. 44-5.

Pg. 69 *".... I lean forward to fix it, explaining with some vexation..."*— Walker, Alice, "Coretta King: Revisited," collected in <u>In Search of our Mothers' Gardens</u>, Harcourt Brace Jovanovich, New York, 1984. Page 151.

Chapter 7

Pg. 110 "Ask the right question..."— This technique is so obscure that Bevel himself doesn't use it any more. In a phone interview, he described the approach he uses now: "1) Ask questions. 2) Find answers. 3) Do work." I find the earlier approach much more powerful.

The reader may wonder why I quote Bevel so often and yet have no examples that involve him, except for the Selma campaign. The reason is that I could find no mention of these techniques in histories, interviews or in any of Bevel's own writing. Apart from Phillip Bradley I could locate no one who recalled Bevel describing these principles or practicing them. If Mr. Bradley hadn't made note of these concepts and passed them on, they might have disappeared entirely.

Chapter 8

Pg. 110 *"The following story was told by Daniel Gordis, an American rabbi..."*— Gordis, Daniel, "E-Mail From an Anxious State," The NY Times Magazine: September 30, 2001.

Bibliography

Almann, Stuart A. Social Communication among Primates. Chicago: UC Press, 1967.

Branch, Taylor. Parting the Waters: America in the King Years, 1954-63. New York: Simon & Schuster, 1988.

Branch, Taylor. Pillar of Fire: America in the King Years, 1963- 65. New York: Simon & Schuster, 1998.

Davis, George, and Glegg Watson. Black Life in Corporate America. Garden City, NY: Anchor/Doubleday 1979.

DeWaal, Franz. Chimpanzee Politics: Power and Sex among the Apes. New York: Harper, Collins 1983

DeWaal, Franz and F.B.M. DeWaal. Peacemaking Among the Primates. Boston: Harvard University Press 1989.

Drucker, Peter F. The Effective Executive. New York: Harper & Row 1967.

Elgin, Suzette Haden. The Gentle Art of Verbal Self Defense. Dorset, 1980.

Elkins, Michael. Families under the Influence: changing alcoholic patterns. New York: Norton Press, 1984.

Friedrich, Otto. "Appeasement at Munich—and the way to war." Smithsonian Magazine: Nov 1988.

Gordis, Daniel, "E-Mail From an Anxious State," The NY Times Magazine: September 30, 2001.

Gottman, John, Ph.D., & Nan Silver. Why Marriages Succeed or Fail: What You Can Learn from Breakthrough Research to Make Your Marriage Last. New York: Simon & Schuster, 1993.

Halberstam, David. The Children. New York: Random House, 1998.

Harragan, Betty Lehan, <u>Games Mother Never Taught You</u>, Warner
  Books, New York, 1977.

Harre, Rom, and Vernon Reynolds. <u>The Meaning of Primate Signals</u>.
  Cambridge: Cambridge UP, 1984.

Helgesen, Sally. <u>The Female Advantage: Women's Ways of Leadership</u>.
  Doubleday Currency, New York, 1990.

Henley, Nancy M. <u>Body Politics: Power, Sex & Nonverbal Communica-
  tion</u>. New York: Simon & Schuster, 1977.

James, Will. "The Breed of 'Em," from Cow Country, 1927. Collected in
  <u>Literature</u>, McDougal, Littell, Evanston, IL, 1987.

Jolly, Alison. <u>The Evolution of Primate Behavior</u>. New York: The
  Macmillian Company, 1972.

Kotulak, Ronald. "Tracking down the monster within us," <u>Chicago
  Tribune</u> December 12, 1993: 1, 22- 23.

Kochman, Thomas. <u>Black and White Styles in Conflict</u>. Chicago: U of C
  Press 1981.

"A Lens on Matrimony," <u>U.S. News & World Report</u> February 21, 1994:
  66- 69.

Ludwig, Arnold M. <u>Understanding the Alcoholic's Mind: the nature
  of craving and how to control it</u>. New York: Grove Press, 1971.

Machiavelli, Niccolo. <u>The Prince</u>. Chicago: Great Books Foundation
  1955.

Maple, Terry L., and Michael P. Hoff. <u>Gorilla Behavior</u>. New York: Van
  Nostrand Reinhold, 1982.

Newton, Nanci. "Body language." Unpublished essay, Madison, WI,
  1984.

Notarius, Cliff, and Howard Markham. <u>We Can Work It Out: How to
  Solve Conflicts, Save Your Marriage, and Strengthen Your Love for
  Each Other</u>. New York: Perigee, 1994.

Powledge, Fred. <u>Free at Last?: The Civil Rights Movement and the People
  who Made it</u>. Boston: Little, Brown and Company, 1991.

Satir, V. Stochowiak & Toschman. <u>Helping Families to Change</u>. New
  York: Bronson, 1975.

Satir, Virginia. The New Peoplemaking. Science and Behavior Books, 1988.

Scheflen, Albert E., M.D., with Alice Scheflen. Body Language and Social Order. Englewood Cliffs, NJ: Prentice-Hall, 1972.

Shreeve, James. "The Brain the Misplaced its Body," Discover May 1995: 82-91

Steiner, Clause. Games Alcoholics Play: the analysis of life scripts. Grove Press, 1971.

Strum, Shirley. Almost Human. New York: Random House, 1987.

Tannen, Deborah, Ph. D. That's Not What I Meant! New York: William Morrow 1984.

Tannen, Deborah, Ph. D. You Just Don't Understand: Men and Women in Conversation. New York: William Morrow 1989.

Walker, Alice, "Coretta King: Revisited," collected in In Search of our Mothers' Gardens. Harcourt Brace Jovanovich, New York, 1984.

Wilmot, William W. and Joyce L. Hocker. Interpersonal Conflict. McGraw-Hill, 2001. 6th edition.

Woititz, Janet Geringer, Ed.D. Adult Children of Alcoholics. Health Communications, Inc. 1983, 1990.

Index

To learn more, share success stories or order more copies of
Conflict Unraveled, please visit our website at:

www.PivotPointPress.com